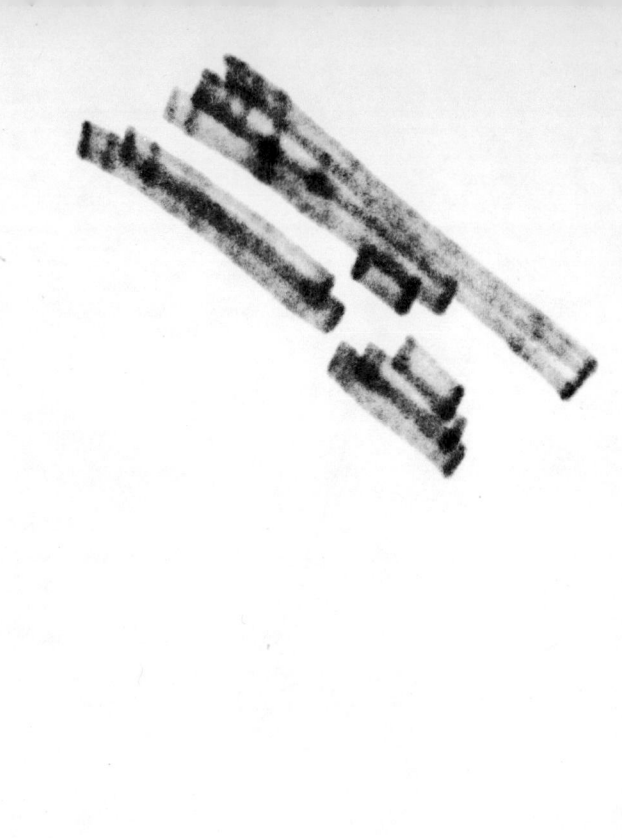

Looking at Art

TORII KIYOMASU. Angry Actor.
Fogg Art Museum,
Harvard University,
Ross Collection.

Alice Elizabeth Chase

LOOKING AT ART

ILLUSTRATED

Thomas Y. Crowell Company
New York

BY THE AUTHOR

Famous Paintings: An Introduction to Art for Young People
Famous Artists of the Past
Looking at Art

The author wishes to thank the following organizations for permission to reproduce the illustrations listed below:

Figures 6, 7, 18, 37, 44, 50, 59, 60, 76, 79, 81, Alinari-Art Reference Bureau. Figures 8, 42, 49, 71, 78, 100, 101, 102, 112, 113, 114, Yale University Art Gallery. Figures 14, 28, 92, 107, 108, 109, Museum of Modern Art. Figures 12, 61, 77, 83, Giraudon, Paris. Figures 2, 3, 16, 17, 34, 56, courtesy, the Trustees of the British Museum. Figures 5, 11, 23, 63, courtesy, Museum of Fine Arts, Boston. Figures 45, 65, 75, 94, 95, courtesy, the Trustees, the National Gallery, London. Figure 88, by permission of the Syndics of the Fitzwilliam Museum, Cambridge. Figure 51, courtesy, the Smithsonian Institution, Freer Gallery of Art, Washington, D.C. Figure 24, copyright, the Frick Collection, New York. Figure 105, © SPADEM 1966 by French Reproduction Rights, Inc. Figure 33, from Newberry, *Beni Hasan*, courtesy, Routledge & Kegan Paul, Ltd., London.

Copyright © 1966 by Alice Elizabeth Chase
All rights reserved. No part of this book may
be reproduced in any form, except by a reviewer,
without the permission of the publisher.
Designed by Bert Clarke
Manufactured in the United States of America
Published in Canada by Fitzhenry & Whiteside Limited, Toronto
Library of Congress Catalog Card No. 66-11947
ISBN 0-690-50869-7
3 4 5 6 7 8 9 10

To Roberta

Contents

1 What Is a Work of Art?   *1*

2 The Artist Looks at a Subject   *5*

3 The Artist Looks at the View   *19*

4 The Artist Looks at People and Space   *35*

5 The Artist Studies the Human Figure   *54*

6 The Artist Creates His Picture   *72*

7 The Artist in the Twentieth Century   *88*

Index   *117*

1. What Is a Work of Art?

Do you own a camera? The chances are you do, but if you have had your camera for several years perhaps you no longer use it much—just get it out for special occasions like family parties or trips. The pictures you take remind you of people and events. Some of them may be quite good, but some are out of focus, too dark or too light, some crooked. You had fun taking them, but you really aren't much interested any more. You seldom look at them.

Or, on the other hand, you may have grown more and more interested in photography. You may have learned about the mechanics, and especially how to select and arrange material to make a satisfying picture. The results have been good and you enjoy the pictures partly because something in them stirs you every time you look: the branches of a tree and their twisted shadows on the snow, for instance, or the jagged profile of a face against the rectangular space of a bright window.

The casual snapshot and the successfully selected and arranged photograph were both, of course, made with the camera, but one took little skill or thought, while the other called for planning and imagination. The difference in the amount of pleasure you get out of the two is the difference between being merely reminded of something, and the deeper satisfaction of having created something. For the second kind of photograph you were not just handling a machine; you were using the machine as a tool, in somewhat the same way a painter uses his brush, to produce the picture that your mind and eye envisioned. You were creating a work of art.

A work of art may be produced in music, poetry, sculpture, architecture, painting, and many other fields besides photography. Its first essential is that it be *created by man*. It is not nature, or the mechanical record of nature. A bird's song, a sunset, a flower, or a rock may be supremely beautiful, but these are not works of art. They can become works of art when man does something to them—when he picks flowers and arranges them in a vase, or when he brings the rock into his garden; when he selects the view for his photograph, or translates what he has heard or seen into music or painting. In these activities he has used his mind and imagination, has made decisions and choices, and is thus creating.

But creations are not always works of art. They may be merely useful. The second essential of a work of art is that it be *more* than useful, that something be added for pure enjoyment. Inventors and mechanics create, so do cooks and seamstresses. When the invention not only works but is pleasing to the eye or ear, when the meal is not only nourishing but good, the dress both warm and pretty, then the creation may be in its own way a work of art. One of the measures of its success and importance as a work of art is the kind of enjoyment it arouses. Is it short-lived, like a sweet taste, or deep and long-lasting?

The third essential of a work of art is that it be the product of *skill*. Skills are of many different kinds and degrees. It takes skill to make a good cake, to take a good photograph, to paint a picture. Skill is acquired by training, practice, and patience. When a person does well whatever he may be trying to do, he has skill.

No one of these essentials by itself makes a work of art. All three must join together. Something created may be stupid and pointless—a scribble, for instance. Enjoyment may come merely from recognizing the subject of a poor photograph. Superb skill, as in engraving a poem on the head of a pin, may be used foolishly. And even if you have all three essentials in a work, it may fail as a work of *art*. For above and beyond these qualities that can be put into words, and more important than all of them, is the fourth essential: something about a work of art that makes you stop and look or listen, and go back again and again, sometimes almost holding your breath. "Art," someone has said, "is a wonder thing."

This book will deal chiefly with paintings, although some sculptures and prints will be included. They have been produced with many different tools and materials, for many different purposes. In each case the artist has ideas which he wants to transmit. He selects from what he sees; he adds, subtracts, adjusts, emphasizes. Figuring out what he was trying to do and why he chose to do it in his particular way is part of the pleasure of looking at works of art.

Figure 1. Walking Lion. Photograph by Robert H. Minton. New York, The American Museum of Natural History.

2. The Artist Looks at a Subject

Some of the different things that artists may try to say about a subject become clear with a study and comparison of different paintings and sculptures of one theme. Consider, for example, the *lion* in art.

Few people in our own time or in the past have seen a lion in the wild, but people seem always to have had ideas about him. The dictionary says that a lion is "a large meat-eating animal of the cat family, having a tufted tail and (in the male) a shaggy mane." But there is more to the lion than this. He is strong and fierce; he moves gracefully, quietly, quickly; he is clever and wily; his roar is loud and frightening. His yellow-brown color and the shaggy mane framing his face suggested to ancient man the rays of the sun, and caused the lion to be regarded as a sun symbol. Because of his size, dignity, strength, and fierceness, he has been called "the king of beasts."

Look first at a photograph of a lion roaming free in the plains of Africa (*Figure 1*). Some of the facts are clear: he is large, he is obviously catlike; he has a tufted tail and a thick mane. Perhaps we could guess his strength from the muscles that show (though they are not too clear), but other characteristics—fierceness, grace, speed, majesty—are not at all evident here. The camera tells us exactly the way the lion looked at a given moment in a certain light. It has made an interesting record.

An artist would have watched the lion a long time in different postures and lights. He would then, probably, have gone to his studio, have selected from memory and emphasized those features that made clear what he felt was important about the lion—things that may not show at all in the photograph. If a group of artists had been watching together, the pictures they produced might have been entirely different from the photograph and from each other, for each artist would have seen and recorded those particular characteristics which impressed him. Similarly varied are the representations of lions throughout history.

More than twenty-five hundred years ago an unknown artist carved lion hunts in relief on the stone walls of an Assyrian palace. He showed the facts of the hunt. The king could not risk his life in the wilds, but sent his men into the jungle to capture lions and bring them back in cages. Then, when the monarch was ready, a lion was released.

The artist must have watched this happening (*Figure 2*). He observed the fury of the beast when it was let out of its cage—its snarling mouth, flattened ears, lowered head. He simplified the hair of the mane into precise diamond-shaped blocks. He knew little about a lion's anatomy, but he knew that it was heavy and muscular—a dangerous beast when, after days in a cage, it was suddenly freed to face its human enemies. The power of the representation lies in the artist's ability to select exactly what was necessary to tell this important fact.

Farther along the wall is a lion (*Figure 3*), mortally wounded by an arrow in his lung, coughing his life out with the blood which streams from his mouth. It is a terrible figure, yet moving, and one cannot escape the thought that the artist felt, and wanted his audience to feel, the tragedy of the great beast in this, his final humiliation.

Neither fierceness nor tragedy belong to the lion (*Figure 4*) which was one of two long lines molded in the brick walls bordering a road leading to a temple gate in ancient Babylon. The snarling mouth has become a fixed mask, the mane and muscles a decorative pattern. Between the walls with these rows of lions, priests and worshipers in procession made their way toward the temple. Their slow, stately movement was reinforced by the long, smooth, undulating line from the top of the head of one lion, along its back and down his tail, where it is flipped

Figure 2. UNKNOWN ARTIST, ASSYRIAN (C. 650 B.C.). Release of the Lion, Relief from Nineveh. London, British Museum.

Figure 3. UNKNOWN ARTIST, ASSYRIAN (C. 650 B.C.). Dying Lion, Relief from Nineveh. London, British Museum.

Figure 4. UNKNOWN ARTIST, BABYLONIAN (C. 550 B.C.). Procession of Lions, from the Ishtar Gate, Babylon. Berlin, National Museum.

up to start again with the head of the next in line. Look back to *Figure 1* and notice the dullness of the line along the lion's back. By lifting the head and tail the Babylonian artist gained rhythm and majesty.

The lion of *Figure 5* was made by a Greek sculptor about 575 B.C. probably for a grave monument. The artist's concern was for dignity and watchfulness. Like the Assyrian and Babylonian masters of *Figures 2, 3,* and *4,* he had a feeling for pattern. The hair on the top of the head rises in flame-like locks, while that on the leg lies in a sort of braid. The forelegs are muscular, the mouth open, the eyes alert, but strength and fierceness are not nearly so important as the formal, decorative presence of the stone beast, a calm and dignified guardian. Sitting or crouching, lions still stand guard over buildings and monuments all over the world, from the Imperial Palace in Peiping to Trafalgar Square in London to the Public Library in New York.

Different again is the lion of *Figure 6* made by a Byzantine artist in the sixth century. The wings show that it is not meant to be an ordinary animal, but the lion of St. Mark, the writer of the second Gospel, who begins his account of the life of Christ with "the voice of one crying in the wilderness." The lion, whose roar is also "a voice . . . in the wilderness," came to be associated with the saint, and to symbolize his Gospel. Thus it was important to suggest the spark of holy fire in the lion's eyes, the spiritual inspiration of the Gospel in his flame-like mane and vital pose.

A lion was linked with another saint, Jerome, who in the fifth century translated the Bible into Latin. His story was em-

Figure 5. UNKNOWN ARTIST, GREEK (C. 575 B.C.). Seated Lion, Probably a Tomb Figure. Boston, Museum of Fine Arts.

Figure 6. UNKNOWN ARTIST, BYZANTINE (VI Century A.D.). Lion of St. Mark. Venice, Piazzetta di San Marco.

bellished with a legend which said that once when he was praying in the wilderness a lion limped up to him with a thorn in its foot. The saint extracted the thorn and the lion became his friend for life. A lion, therefore, almost always appears with St. Jerome. The Venetian artist Vittore Carpaccio painted him as a harmless, friendly creature wearing a benign smile as the saint introduces him to his terrified colleagues (*Figure 7*).

The sculptor of *Figure 6* probably cared little about the real appearance of a lion, but in the Renaissance, artists were deeply concerned with representing things correctly. They studied anatomy and sketched from models. But lions were few. The lion in *Figure 8* by Albrecht Dürer of Nuremberg seems to combine the characteristics Dürer had seen in works of art,

Figure 7. VITTORE CARPACCIO, ITALIAN (c. 1460–1522). St. Jerome Returning with the Lion. Venice, Scuola di S. Giorgio Schiavone.

Figure 8. ALBRECHT DÜRER, GERMAN (1471–1526). St. Jerome in His Study, Engraving. New Haven, Yale University Art Gallery.

with his study of the hair and muscles of the family cat. Later, Dürer mentions in his diary that on a trip to Antwerp he saw a live lion and made sketches of it (*Figure 9*) so that when he next wanted to include one in a painting he could be more accurate.

II

Figure 9. ALBRECHT DÜRER, GERMAN (1471–1526). Lion Drawn from Life. Berlin, Kupferstichkabinett.

A touch of humor pervades the Japanese lions (*Figure 10*) from a twelfth-century scroll. The open mouth and glaring eyes of the standing beast could be frightening, but joined to the neck with its elegant curls and especially the gaily waving tail, they became mock-heroic. With the next lion, who lifts his hind leg to scratch his ear and closes his eyes like any pet cat or dog, it becomes clear that the artist is suggesting that lions are in many ways no different from other less awesome animals. He painted with swift, accurate brushstrokes, for ink on absorbent paper cannot be corrected. Shadows were left out and the feeling of movement, of the action of muscles, comes from the sensitive and sure outline.

A lion chained is the subject of a sixteenth-century Persian painting (*Figure 11*). Here the artist is concerned not with the inner nature of the beast or any struggle against captivity, but with the curves of his figure: the nose and mouth, the neck, the back, the hind legs, and the reversed curve of the tail. These

Figure 10. TOBA SOJO (Bishop of Toba), JAPANESE (1053–1140). Lions. Kyoto, Kozanji.

smooth, living curves are contrasted sharply with the rigid zigzag of the chain.

By the nineteenth century, scientific curiosity had brought about new attitudes on the part of artists. Lions could be seen safely behind bars in public zoos and people thronged to stare. Artists could stay all day, watching the movements of the great creatures as they paced their cages, played, or rested. Eugène

Figure 11. USTÁD MURÁD, PERSIAN (XVI Century). Chained Lion. Boston, Museum of Fine Arts.

Figure 12. EUGÉNE DELACROIX, FRENCH (1798–1863). Lion Devouring a Rabbit. Paris, Louvre.

Figure 13. ANTOINE LOUIS BARYE, FRENCH (1796–1875). Lion Walking. New York, The Metropolitan Museum of Art, Rogers Fund, 1910.

Figure 14. HENRI ROUSSEAU, FRENCH (1844–1910). The Sleeping Gypsy. New York, Museum of Modern Art.

Delacroix painted one eating its dinner (*Figure 12*). There is nothing noble about its action. It is simply a powerful animal absorbed in satisfying hunger. We see its controlled strength, its energy and vitality.

Antoine Barye, a contemporary of Delacroix, did much the same thing in sculpture, modeling the "big cats" of the zoo in lifelike postures and actions from sketches he had made on the spot. It is interesting to compare Barye's rendering of a walking lion (*Figure 13*) with the photograph of *Figure 1* and with *Figures 2, 4,* and *11*. The similarities in pose are striking, but the differences in handling of detail are significant. The Assyrian, Babylonian, and Persian artists observed the posture and anatomy of lions but translated what they saw into patterns. Barye, a realist, stayed closer to appearance, emphasizing the

15

muscles, especially those of shoulder and back, making the mane look casually shaggy. The lifted head is vigorous and alert; the tail curves gracefully.

While Delacroix and Barye were concerned with how lions really look, Henri Rousseau thought of them as creatures in a fairy tale. His lion (*Figure 14*) is half real, half a stuffed toy with a woolly mane and a bead for an eye. It sniffs at the woman but does not disturb her. She, in her rainbow dress, sleeps deeply in the moonlit desert. No footprints lead to the spot. The picture is a sort of dream fantasy. A French poet, Jean Cocteau, called it "painted poetry."

To Darrel Austin, the lion is powerful, majestic, and dignified, but also mysterious and frightening (*Figure 15*). He paints him in a devastated swamp with damp mists rising, and will-o'-the-wisp lights. Alert, watchful, poised, the creature is ready either to pounce or to take flight. He is not the self-assured king of beasts that so many artists have portrayed, but the true animal, nervous, wary, watchful for the unexpected.

These are only a sampling of the thousands upon thousands of lions that have been produced by artists throughout the centuries. For a scientific record of the appearance of a lion you turn to a photograph. But many people looking at photographs, or seeing a lion in a zoo for the first time, find themselves a little disappointed. Is this because their ideas about lions have been founded on art rather than on science? Are the paintings and sculptures so much more interesting than the reality that the reality is a disappointment? Perhaps it is through works of art that people come to understand what the lion has meant in various times and religions, what inspiration he has furnished to mankind.

Figure 15. DARREL AUSTIN, AMERICAN (1907–   ). Young Lion in Moonlight. New York, Perls Gallery.

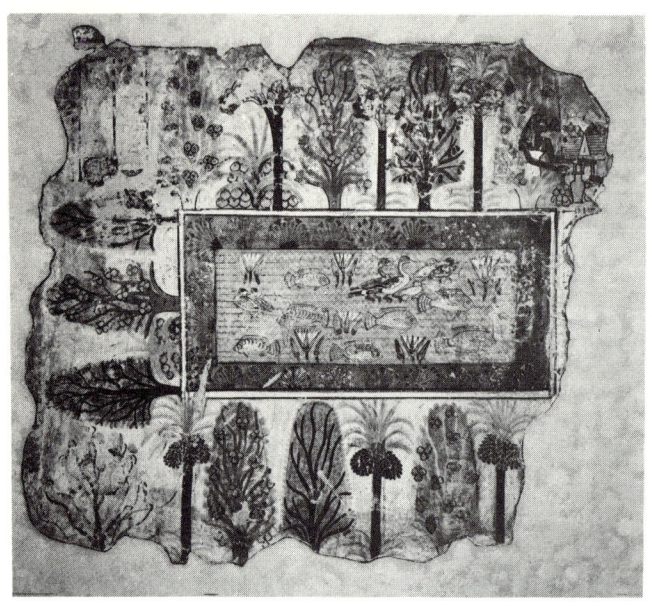

Figure 16. UNKNOWN ARTIST, EGYPTIAN (XVIII Dynasty, c. 1450 B.C.). Garden with Pond from the Tomb of Amenemheb, Thebes. London, British Museum.

Figure 17. UNKNOWN ARTIST, ASSYRIAN (c. 650 B.C.). Landscape (detail), Relief from Nineveh. London, British Museum.

3. The Artist Looks at the View

Looking at a view from a great height, we unconsciously realize that objects nearby are big and clear, their colors bright, while those farther away seem smaller, fainter, and more blurred. Because of dust particles in the air, mountains in the distance appear blue or lavender against the sky.

A camera will record the way things look. But to the artist the representation of a wide and distant view offers a real challenge. He must confine its immensity to the limits of his canvas or wall; he must reduce its size, or take a small section of it. He must *do* something with the landscape to express his ideas about it. Perhaps he will cut out some of its myriad detail, will select and emphasize. He may even try to show that distant objects are not actually smaller than near ones, or mountains really blue. Scenery varies in different parts of the world; ways of looking at it and painting it vary even more.

To an ancient Egyptian artist the important fact about a garden pool was its shape and the creatures swimming in it (*Figure 16*). The scene is not a "view" at all, but a kind of map. The pool was rectangular so he painted a rectangle. Regular zigzag lines symbolize the ripples. Fish and birds are seen most clearly side view so they are shown in profile. Each tree is separate, its species clearly indicated. The painting informs us about the shape of the pond, the wildlife, the trees, rather than showing them to us as they appear.

A landscape detail from a lion-hunting relief of the seventh century B.C. in Assyria also shows things in profile (*Figure 17*). A wooded hill rounds against the sky. Trees and shrubs are seen in silhouette, as are the men and women clambering upward. On top of the hill is a monument with a relief showing the king killing a lion.

Greek artists seem to have used trees and rocks chiefly to

provide a setting for human figures, but ancient Romans enjoyed landscape for other reasons. A returning hero might deck his triumphal procession with banners showing views of the cities and lands he had conquered. The Empress Livia, wife of Augustus, had a "garden room" in which she could enjoy the illusion of being surrounded by a shady wood. Its walls were painted with trees and flowers among which different varieties of birds flew about. Outdoor scenes, usually illustrating a story or poem, adorned the walls of private villas. Framed between painted columns or pilasters, they gave the appearance of windows opening to views of mountains and seas peopled with legendary heroes (*Figure 18*). The landscapes are never real but rather the fanciful imaginings of city dwellers who think of the country as a bright and happy world remote from turmoil. Mists rise from clefts in fantastic mountains and glimpses open into distances where sea and sky meet.

Figure 18. UNKNOWN ARTIST, ROMAN (I Century B.C.). Odysseus in the Land of the Cannibals. Rome, Vatican Library.

Figure 19. TUNG CH'I-CH'ANG, CHINESE (1555–1636). The Ch'ing-pien Mountains. New York, Collection of Wango H. C. Weng.

The Chinese considered landscape the most important of subjects because it suggested both the moods of man and the infinity of God. Often accompanied by a poem, it was painted on paper or silk with the ink and brushes used for writing. The long hand scrolls were meant to be "read" like books, unrolled

21

slowly to reveal one episode after another. Often the only color came from variation in the blackness of the ink.

Mountains such as appear in *Figure 19* seem as fantastic as those of Roman painting, though mountaintops rising out of mist and sharply outlined against the sky are characteristic of Chinese scenery. Different brushstrokes had been established as standard for expressing such things as rocks, tree trunks, foliage, grasses. Mists, sky, and water were sometimes suggested by leaving unpainted areas on the paper. These blank areas help to stir the mood of revery that one often feels in the presence of Chinese landscape painting. "Landscape," said Kuo Hsi in the eleventh century, "is a big thing and should be viewed from a distance in order to grasp the scheme of hill and stream." In the landscape by Tung Ch'i-ch'ang the spectator is high above the view, looking down and across into it. The mountains are outlined with irregular curved strokes, building their curious shapes, dark against light. Each of the varieties of trees that mount the slopes is drawn with its own kind of brushstroke.

Flat gold backgrounds set off the saints of early medieval painting in the West, but by the fifteenth century, increased interest in the world around them led artists, both North and South, to replace the gold with views of fields, mountains, and sky fading to a blue distance. In Italy, landscape was seldom more than a setting for figures and story, but in the North, in the hands of such manuscript illuminators as Hubert van Eyck, the setting was fully as important as the action pictured in it. The "Baptism of Christ" is the subject of a small painting by van Eyck at the bottom of the page of a book (*Figure 20*). Standing in the stream, John pours water over the head of Christ. To the right, people are gathering; in an initial to the left, God presides, sending down the dove of the Holy Spirit on rays of light. The storytelling is adequate, but the event is only an incident in the foreground. The landscape setting is superb. Distant windings of the stream can be traced by the mists that

Figure 20. HUBERT VAN EYCK (?), FLEMISH (c. 1366–1426). Baptism of Christ (detail from the Turin *Hours*). Turin, Museo Civico.

rise from it. Buildings, forest, and riverbank are observed and recorded with minute accuracy. As the river widens toward the foreground, the castle and trees are reflected in its gently moving waters. It was because the medieval thinker saw the presence of God in every detail of nature that the landscape of his own country became a worthy setting for a religious subject. Over and over again in Flemish painting, behind a madonna or a scene of saints and angels, an arch or window opens on a landscape (*Figure 21*). The atmosphere is still, objects and people are clear-cut against the pale blue of the distance. One seems to be looking at something very precious: the serene perfection of God's world.

Although more interested in everyday life around him, Pieter Bruegel in the sixteenth century had a point of view similar to that of the Flemish artists of the previous century. Man with his myriad activities was merely an incident in a great and beautiful world where his daily routine, his joys and griefs,

Figure 21. HANS MEMLING, FLEMISH (1433?-1494). Madonna with Angels. Washington, National Gallery of Art, Andrew Mellon Collection.

Figure 22. PIETER BRUEGEL, FLEMISH (c.1525–1569). Death of Saul at the Battle of Gilboa. Vienna, Kunsthistorisches Museum.

were relatively unimportant. Nowhere does Bruegel make one feel this more than in his "Death of Saul" (*Figure 22*). The armies of Israel are losing the battle to dense hordes of Philistines. Saul and his son and armor-bearer have fled to a cliff-top where, seeing defeat and capture inevitable, father and son have killed themselves. The tragedy is told by tiny figures in the foreground, not centered as one would expect, but far to the left. Beyond the struggle spreads a serene green valley through which a river winds toward a distant city.

A more intimate view of the world appears in seventeenth-century landscape in Holland. The Dutch loved their countryside and liked to paint its broad flat fields for their own sake. They realized too the fascination of sky. Yellow-white clouds piling up against a watery blue sky typical of the Low Countries often occupy more than half of a canvas painted by Jacob

Figure 23. JACOB VAN RUYSDAEL, DUTCH (1625/9–1682). View of Haarlem from the Dunes. Boston, Museum of Fine Arts.

van Ruysdael (*Figure 23*). His modification of tones, his use of sun and shadow, make the fields below stretch on and on.

As landscapes became more popular, artists established a formula by which they could turn them out quickly without bothering to study actual effects of light and air (*Figure 24*).

In the foreground a large tree with people or a cottage was painted dark greenish-brown. Next came a light area, then a dark, then another light, alternating to carry the eye to the distant horizon. In the hands of great artists this formula might be varied with much originality, but its wide acceptance was responsible for the brownish landscapes produced in Europe throughout the eighteenth century.

In the early nineteenth century it became fashionable for English gentlemen to order paintings of their country estates. An accurate record of the house and grounds was, of course, the first essential, and the dull greens and browns of conventional landscape were adequate. But as artists studied the view

Figure 24. MEINDERT HOBBEMA, DUTCH (1638–1709). Village in a Wood with Watermill, among Trees. New York, Frick Collection.

Figure 25. JOHN CONSTABLE, ENGLISH (1776–1834). The White Horse. Washington, National Gallery of Art, Widener Collection.

they became interested in color and atmosphere. John Constable, the most famous English landscapist of this period, used a fresher color, expressing a sense of moisture, of the possibility of growth in grass and trees (*Figure 25*).

It was the detailed and factual landscape of the English school, brightened, sometimes, by color such as Constable's, that was brought to the United States. In the eighteenth century, landscape had seldom been called for except as background for portraits. Settlers in a vast and wild new country did not particularly want to be reminded of the outdoors.

Figure 26. GEORGE INNESS, AMERICAN (1825–1894). On the Delaware River. New York, The Brooklyn Museum.

But by the nineteenth century cities were well established, the nation had secured its independence, and the new patriotism and enthusiasm for America showed itself in an interest in the countryside. Artists painted the Connecticut River Valley, and then, as the population moved westward, the Hudson, the Adirondacks, and finally the prairies and the Rocky Mountains.

To people proud of their nation the facts of the view were important. But even more so was the sense of bigness, of distance, of fertility. In George Inness' "On the Delaware River" (*Figure 26*) one looks down the broad river valley to distant hills. A railroad train coming forward on the left, and tiny men guiding their rafts downstream hint at pioneering into new territory.

Albert Bierstadt went farther west and painted the Rockies, responding to their wildness and majesty. His painting of Mount Corcoran (now Mount Langley) in California (*Figure 27*) shows the lofty peak rising through mists almost to the top of the picture, while storm clouds roll away to the left. A lone bear comes from among the forest's ancient, storm-torn trees down to the water's edge to drink. This is the romantic vision of the great West that delighted the Eastern city dwellers—a vision of wild, lonely grandeur.

Toward the middle of the nineteenth century the wide landscape gave way to a more intimate view of garden, field, or stream. Artists took their easels outdoors and tried to paint what they saw, absorbed in the problem of analyzing and recording effects of light and air. The artist used his eye much as

Figure 27. ALBERT BIERSTADT, AMERICAN (1830–1902). Mount Corcoran (Sierra Nevada). Washington, Corcoran Art Gallery.

Figure 28. VINCENT VAN GOGH, DUTCH (1853–1890). The Starry Night. New York, Museum of Modern Art.

a photographer uses a camera lens—merely to see. But great artists soon realized that a work of art is more than merely a record of what one sees. It is the expression of man's thoughts and feelings. Artists changed and adjusted what they saw in order to present ideas. Vincent van Gogh in his "Starry Night" painted a world stirring with forces that seem to become visible in flame-like cypresses and whirling stars (*Figure 28*).

Figure 29. PAUL CÉZANNE, FRENCH (1839–1906). Mont Sainte-Victoire from Les Lauves. Philadelphia Museum of Art, George W. Elkins Collection.

Paul Cézanne in "Mont Sainte-Victoire" (*Figure 29*) built its shape high against the sky, arranged the fields and houses between the spectator and the distant mountain into ordered blocks of vertical and horizontal brushstrokes which carry one inexorably over the intervening area. It is a real view; it has been photographed from the very spot where Cézanne must have stood. The photograph shows a low and unimpressive mountain. The painting brings us Cézanne's feeling about it. He had trudged every step of the way through the valley many times, and he tried to transmit the sense of the domination of this great mountain-shape as it rose ever larger above him.

All of us have experienced the thrill of looking at a view. Does the artist's painting of such a scene merely recall our delight? It can also show us new ways of seeing, can sharpen our perception, and can give us a deeper and richer sense of the relation of nature and man.

Figure 30. UNKNOWN ARTIST, EGYPTIAN (C. 1411–1375 B.C.). Funeral Procession, Wall Painting from the Tomb of Ramose, Thebes. Photograph by Egyptian Expedition. New York, The Metropolitan Museum of Art.

Figure 31. UNKNOWN ARTIST, EGYPTIAN (C. 1411–1375 B.C.). Female Mourners, Wall Painting from the Tomb of Ramose, Thebes. Photograph by Egyptian Expedition. New York, The Metropolitan Museum of Art.

4. The Artist Looks at People and Space

Photographing a group of people in action always poses problems: people get in each other's way; one person's shoulder hides part of another person; shadows blot out details. Moviemakers meet the situation by using lights and by rehearsing their actors so that each sits and stands in exactly the right position; but the amateur photographer seldom has time to pose his group so carefully, and if he does, the result often looks stiff and unnatural.

Artists have tried various solutions for these problems. The Egyptian made the human figure into a sort of map—the face profile, the shoulders usually front view, the legs side view. People side by side may be overlapped, but they have no thickness. In the funeral procession (*Figure 30*) from the Tomb of Ramose, bodies are distinguished from one another by being painted alternately light and dark. A study of the female mourners (*Figure 31*) from the same tomb reveals that there are not enough feet to go around. The heads on the top row have shoulders and arms but no bodies; they are as big as or bigger than the people below them, yet being overlapped by the two lower rows, they are obviously intended to be farther away. Representing things in this way may not be true to what the eye sees, but it often shows what is going on better than a photograph could. Egyptian picture writing (hieroglyphic) accompanies the scene, filling blank spaces on the walls. One "reads" the picture almost as though it, too, were picture writing.

How clearly this method of representation can tell what is happening is shown in a detail of a harvesting scene (*Figure 32*). Two men have heaped a basket with wheat. One holds the end

Figure 32. UNKNOWN ARTIST, EGYPTIAN (C. 1422–1411 B.C.). Harvesting Scene, Wall Painting from the Tomb of Nahkt, Thebes. Photograph by Harry Burton. New York, The Metropolitan Museum of Art.

Figure 33. UNKNOWN ARTIST, EGYPTIAN (XII Dynasty). Wrestlers, Wall Painting from the Tomb of Ameni, Beni Hasan.

of a pole which passes over the lid, while the other leaps into the air to exert the pressure of his weight to squeeze down the grain so that he can tie the cover with a rope. A woman at the right gathers into her little basket the ears that have been dropped by the reapers. Although there is some suggestion of foreshortening in the shoulders of the woman and of the man at the left, the objects and actions are rendered chiefly in profile. Often the entire wall of a tomb or temple was covered with strips of scenes showing the activities of daily life. In a tomb at Beni Hasan (*Figure 33*), wrestling holds recount the contest play by play.

A similar profile system was used in ancient Mesopotamia. In the view of the Assyrian King Assurnasirpal's encampment and stables (*Figure 34*), that once decorated the walls of his palace at Nimrud, we see the circular camp at left as a diagram, towers jutting from its walls. Inside, it is divided into four pie-shaped sections in which people engage in cooling wine, slaughtering, cooking. In the center of the relief, horses are drinking at a trough. They overlap each other, yet their feet

Figure 34. UNKNOWN ARTIST, ASSYRIAN (IX Century B.C.). King Assurnasirpal's Encampment and Stables, Alabaster Relief from the Throne Room of the Northwest Palace at Nimrud. London, British Museum.

37

are all on one level. The one above, which is being rubbed down by a groom, may be intended to be farther back in the group though it is the same size as those below. That the artist had not thought of representing space visually is indicated by the groom's right foot, oddly placed as though in front of one horse and on the neck of another. On the right, receiving bound prisoners (whose bodies overlap each other), is an official, made large to emphasize his importance. Two of the four sides of a canopy show behind him. These are erected vertically, not drawn in plan like the walls of the camp. The front posts are ornamented with carved ibexes. Above the prisoners is another figure, also larger than they, perhaps a priest, facing two creatures, part man, part lion, who are probably gods. Thus in this short panel the artist employed both the map space of the camp and the vertical space of people, animals, and canopy. He suggested depth by overlapping; he used large size to signify importance. All these are ways of giving information about people and places.

Since no Greek wall paintings of the classical period have come down to us, it is from the decorations on pottery that we learn how the Greeks handled figures in action. Like the Egyptians, they had usually shown people in profile, but by the fifth century B.C. bodies were being drawn to indicate the third dimension. In *Figure 35* the shoulders of Heracles are shown correctly from the side, while those of Athena are turned in an accurate three-quarter view. Most interesting here, however, is the wine jar from which Athena pours into Heracles' cup. This faces out, its body a foreshortened oval. In a wrestling scene (*Figure 36*) the trainer is twisted awkwardly, face side view and shoulders front view, but the wrestlers are quite accurately foreshortened; the right knee of the central figure is in front of his ankle and toes, and the shoulders and hips of the man being thrown are drawn the way they look.

In none of the works shown so far has shadow been used to suggest solidity or depth in space. But certain mosaics and

Figure 35. DURIS, GREEK (V Century B.C.). Heracles and Athena, Vase Painting. Munich, Museum Antiker Kleinkunst.

Figure 36. UNKNOWN ARTIST, GREEK (V Century B.C.). Wrestling Scene, Vase Painting. Paris, Cabinet des Medailles.

Figure 37. DIOSKOURIDES, GREEK (?) (II Century B.C., possibly after a IV Century B.C. model). Street Musicians, Mosaic. Naples, Museo Nationale.

paintings found in Italy that date from the second or first century B.C. model figures in light and shade. One of these (*Figure 37*) shows street musicians: a masked woman blowing a double flute, a man with cymbals, and another with a tambourine. Not only are their feet, hands, and arms correctly foreshortened, but they stand on ground having visible depth, and

40

they cast shadows on it and on the wall behind. Their bodies are given substance by light coming from the right which throws their backs into shadow. There is evidence that this mosaic derives from an earlier Greek painting, and that the beginning of modeling in light and shade can be attributed to the Greeks.

When artists try to show things as they look, they come up against the problem of perspective. We noted in the landscapes of Chapter 3 how things look smaller at a distance than close to, and how colors seem brighter in the foreground, bluer in the distance. Edges of a road seem to slope together. A railroad track extends into the distance until its rails seem to come together at a point on the horizon (*Figure 38*). The ties, which are far apart at our feet, appear closer and closer together as well as shorter and shorter as they move into the distance. The same thing happens to the telephone poles along the track; they too disappear at a vanishing point on the horizon where earth and sky meet. This horizon is our eye level. The near wall of a building that faces us is bounded by parallel horizontals and verticals. Its side walls diminish as they go back. If the

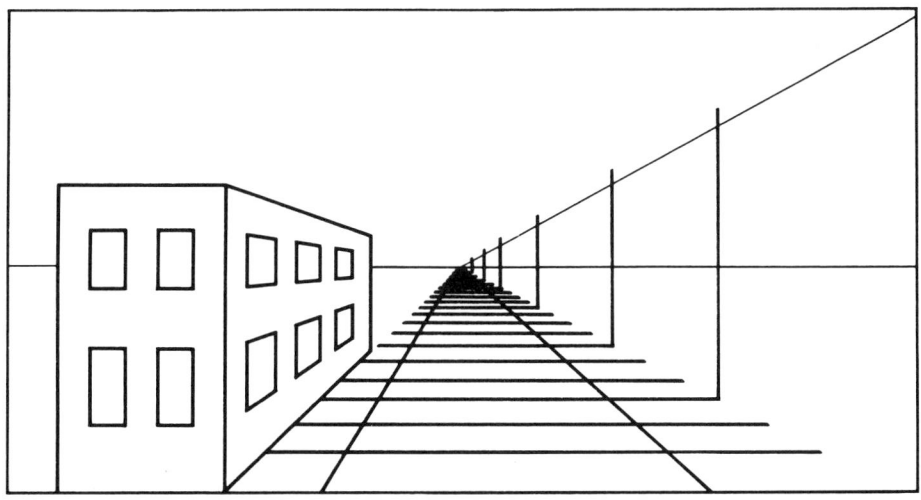

Figure 38. Diagram: Railroad track showing vanishing-point perspective.

Figure 39. Diagram: Building seen from the corner to show two vanishing points.

building is seen from an angle, its verticals are still parallel, but its horizontals recede to two vanishing points, one to the right, the other to the left on the horizon line (*Figure 39*).

People must have observed these facts in ancient times, but many did not stop to analyze them and artists were not concerned about them. An ancient Egyptian might have said: "But the man in the distance is *not* smaller than the man nearby; the side walls of that house are *not* shorter at the far end than they are at this end. What I *see* is not true. I will paint things as I know them to be, not as they look."

But the ancient Greeks and Romans *did* want their art to show things as they looked. They had observed the tendency of parallel lines to come together, as in the diagram of the railroad track, but apparently they did not work out a system of vanishing-point perspective. In *Figure 40*, a Roman wall painting of buildings, the architecture looks all right, but the edges of the receding walls meet at different points along a vertical line, not at a vanishing point (see diagram, *Figure 41*). The perspective satisfies the casual glance but is not scientific.

Figure 40. UNKNOWN ARTIST, ROMAN (I Century B.C.). View of Buildings, Wall Painting from Boscoreale. New York, The Metropolitan Museum of Art, Rogers Fund, 1903.

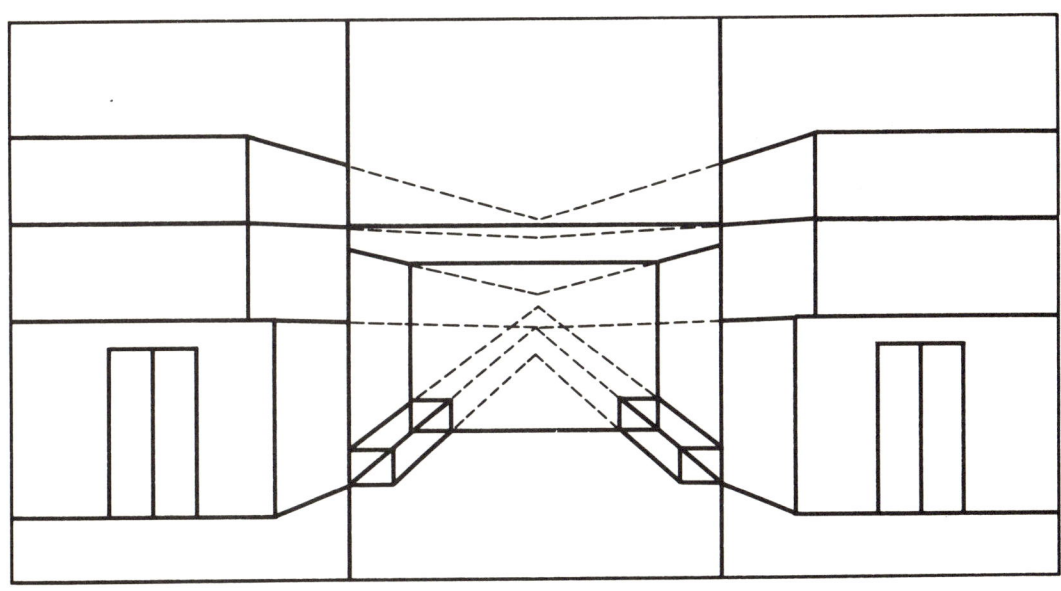

Figure 41. Diagram: To show Roman method of systematizing space.

Figure 42. SASSETTA (Stefano di Giovanni), ITALIAN (1392–1450). St. Anthony Tormented by Demons. New Haven, Yale University Art Gallery, James Jackson Jarves Collection.

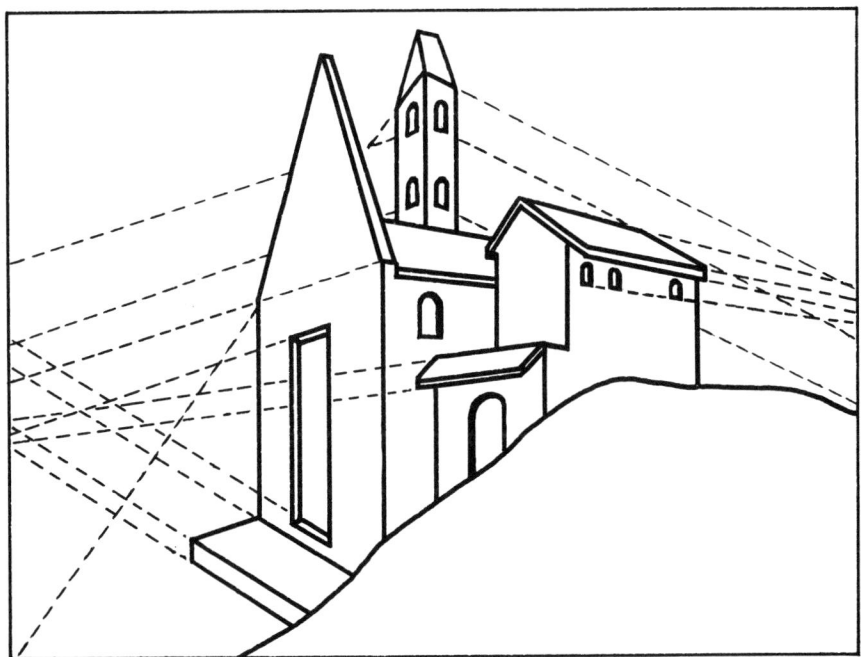

Figure 43. Diagram: Building in Figure 42, showing multiple vanishing points.

The ideas of the Middle Ages about perspective are suggested in a book on art written by an Italian painter, Cennino Cennini, about 1400:

> Put in a building by this system: that the moldings which you make at the top of the building should slant downward from the edge next to the roof; the molding in the middle of the building, halfway up the face, must be quite level and even; the molding at the base of the building underneath must slant upward, in the opposite sense to the upper molding which slants downward.

There is no indication of the direction of these slanting lines beyond the simple one that those above slant down, those below, up. The points at which they meet are many and not on a single horizon line (see *Figure 42* and diagram, *Figure 43*).

In the fifteenth century, artists began to study vision scientifically, searching for the laws that govern the relations of sizes and shapes as they appear in space. The discovery and formulation of these laws challenged the Italian architects Filippo Brunelleschi and Leon Battista Alberti, and such painters as Paolo Uccello, Piero della Francesca, and Leonardo da Vinci.

Figure 44. PAOLO UCCELLO, ITALIAN (1396–1475). Room from a Series of Scenes from the Life of St. James. Urbino, Ducal Palace.

Figure 45. PAOLO UCCELLO, ITALIAN (1396–1475). The Battle of San Romano. London, National Gallery.

Figure 46. ALBRECHT DÜRER, GERMAN (1471–1526). Drawing a Lute, Woodcut. New York, The Metropolitan Museum of Art.

Uccello is said to have annoyed his wife by murmuring over and over, "Oh, thou sweet Perspective." In *Figure 44* he painted the interior of a shop, its three walls, ceiling beams, and tiled floor carefully receding to a vanishing point exactly in the middle of the picture. In his "Battle of San Romano" (*Figure 45*) Uccello tried to foreshorten the lances, armor, and the fallen man with similar scientific accuracy, and relate all to a vanishing point in the distance. That things do not look quite "right" is not only because he made errors, but also because it is not possible to limit vision to any one scientific scheme. We have two eyes; we move our heads; we shift our glance; we walk around. What is exactly accurate for a single eye fixed at a point is not accurate for the restless human eye.

The sixteenth-century German Albrecht Dürer left drawings and diagrams to show how he believed scientific accuracy could be attained. The lute in *Figure 46* has been laid on a table and a frame with a piece of tracing paper has been set up vertically on the same level. A nail in the wall behind the artist represents his eye, and a string stretched from the nail to a point on the instrument stands for the eye's glance. Where this string would go through the paper in the vertical frame, a dot was made. When there were enough dots, as on the white sheet which has been swung back for us to see, lines were drawn connecting them and the artist had an exact record of how the lute would look viewed from the spot where the nail is.

This system works reasonably well for small objects at a convenient distance (although it allows for only one eye), but when things are very close, or at the sides of vision, we have other problems. *Figure 47* shows what the camera's single fixed eye sees when focused on a reclining man from a point close above his feet. We are amused at the distortion. Our minds make unconscious adjustments and would have automatically corrected such a view for us, but the camera shows what we really see. Take the picture from farther away and the cam-

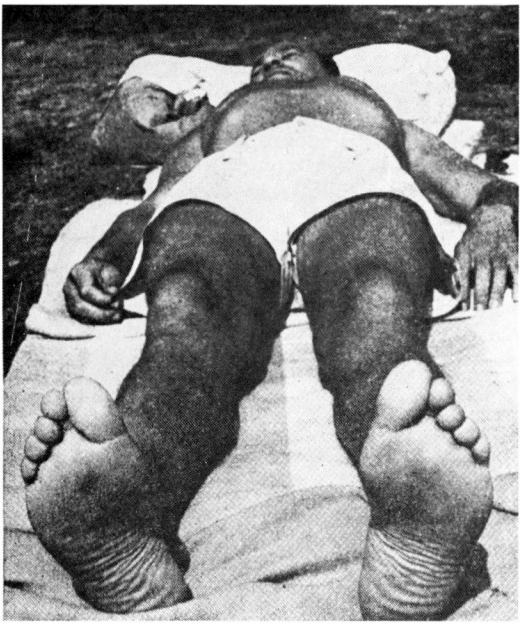

Figure 47. Photograph of a Man Lying Down.

48

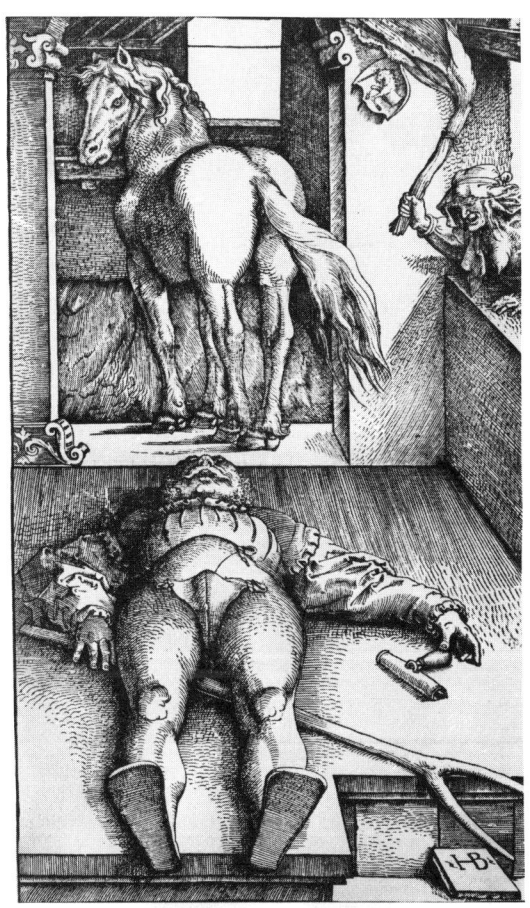

Figure 48. HANS BALDUNG (called GRÜN), GERMAN (1475–1545). The Groom Bewitched, Woodcut. New Haven, Yale University Art Gallery.

era's foreshortening would look accurate. Hans Baldung, called Grün, a contemporary of Dürer, explored some of these problems in "The Groom Bewitched" (*Figure 48*), which shows a man lying on the stable floor while a horse, back to, stands farther away against a window.

Renaissance innovators became so fascinated with perspective and foreshortening that they tried many experiments with the relationship between the spectator and the picture. Andrea Mantegna's scenes from the life of St. James in the Church of the Eremitani in Padua (*Figure 49*) are placed on the wall above the eye level of a person of average height. The viewer looks up into the arch through which the saint is about to pass

49

on his way to martyrdom. The vanishing point is *below* the painting. The underside of the foot of the soldier in the middle shows over the edge of the street, and the feet of the more distant figures are cut off by the bottom of the picture.

By the end of the seventeenth century the mastery of perspective made possible fantastically skillful compositions of figures in space. The ceiling of the Church of St. Ignazio in

Figure 49. ANDREA MANTEGNA, ITALIAN (1431–1506). St. James Led to Martyrdom. Padua, Church of the Eremitani.

Figure 50. ANDREA POZZI, ITALIAN (1692–1709). St. Ignazio Entering Heaven. Rome, Church of S. Ignazio.

Rome, painted by Andrea Pozzi (*Figure 50*), seems to push through the architecture to open a view to heaven itself. One gazes up, past innumerable saints and angels whose legs dangle over the edge of painted architectural moldings, to incredible heights of painted clouds. Crowds of people, amazingly foreshortened, join in an ecstasy of adoration. If the modern spectator finds himself a little bored by the painting, it is partly because taste changes. Today we seek something other than superb technical skill.

The Chinese and Japanese use what is called "isometric perspective." In this scheme lines that are parallel continue parallel and do not come together at a vanishing point. This

51

Figure 51. KATSUKAWA, JAPANESE (1726–1792). Women Airing Books. Washington, Freer Gallery of Art.

is the case in the eighteenth-century painting of "Women Airing Books" (*Figure 51*). We are looking down on rooms and courtyards that open into each other but are not presented through vanishing-point perspective. We are so used to thinking of diagonal parallel lines coming together that when they don't we get the impression, as here, that they are spreading apart. The Japanese artist uses no shadows and does not observe the laws of foreshortening, but he carefully follows his own system, and with a little practice, we learn to understand the scene clearly.

This Oriental method of representing space is used by architects in the Western world to show the structure of a building better than vanishing-point perspective will. In *Figure 52* one can see how well the isometric view serves the artist's purpose, making it possible to see the inside as well as the outside of the building.

In this chapter we have seen artists handling space in the flat profile method, through overlapping, through modeling in light and shade, through cast shadow. We have observed perspective and foreshortening; we have noted the Oriental isometric scheme. It becomes clear that there is no one "right" way to represent space. Each of the systems we have looked at has points in its favor. Vanishing-point perspective is what we are used to, is truer to *what the eye sees*, but there are things that can be shown more truly by another system.

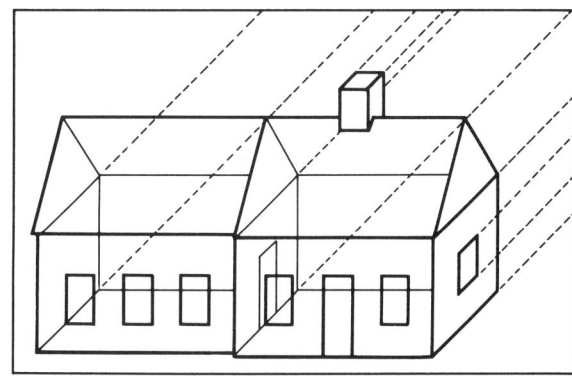

Figure 52. Diagram: Isometric drawing of a building.

5. The Artist Studies the Human Figure

Of all the subjects represented by photographers and artists the most common is the human figure. Turn the pages of most picture magazines and you find photographs of people, old or young, still or moving. Often they are shown because they are of interest as individuals—people who are making news. But the reason for the picture may be simply the beauty of the human body, or the muscular coordination visible in a well-developed figure in action. The photographer experiments with the lights in his studio to emphasize contours and masses, or he works outdoors with special lenses and high-speed film to catch the action of a fraction of a second. His camera's eye is so much quicker than the human eye that he has made significant discoveries about how things move.

To artists, depicting the human body offers a challenge which can be met in a variety of ways, depending on their ideas of what is important about people. The Egyptians, for instance, maintained throughout three thousand years the profile rendering of the human body which we have noted. Yet they often included bits of accurate anatomical detail. The face, the shoulders, the kneecaps of Hesi-Re, carved in relief on a wooden panel of 2700 B.C., seem to have bones and muscles under the skin (*Figure 53*). Egyptian artists also had an eye for the unusual or for details that characterized an individual or a class. The blind musician (*Figure 54*) was rendered with little concern for correct representation of the squatting posture or the fingers plucking the strings, but the artist took pains to show the sagging stomach muscles that mark a person who spends most of his time sitting, and has made the viewer touchingly aware of blindness by leaving out the eye altogether. The

Figure 53. UNKNOWN ARTIST, EGYPTIAN
(C. 2700 B.C.). Relief of Hesi-Re, Wood.
Cairo, Art Museum.

Figure 54. UNKNOWN ARTIST, EGYPTIAN (C. 1422–1411 B.C.).
Blind Musician, Wall Painting from the Tomb of Nahkt,
Thebes. Photograph by Egyptian Expedition. New York,
The Metropolitan Museum of Art.

Figure 55. UNKNOWN ARTIST, EGYPTIAN (C. 1375–1350 B.C.). Akhenaten and Nefertiti. New York, Brooklyn Museum, Wilbour Collection.

curiously long head, neck, and pointed chin that characterize the Pharaoh Akhenaten and his wife, who ruled in the fourteenth century B.C., may be partly an artist's invention, but were probably also derived from actual appearance (*Figure 55*).

Mesopotamian conventions for representing the human body included exaggerated kneecaps and leg and arm muscles (*Figure 56*). Wall paintings from the Cretan palace at Knossos and figures inlaid in gold on dagger blades from Mycenae on the Greek mainland indicate that in preclassical Greece broad shoulders and narrow waists were emphasized in youthful figures (*Figure 57*).

Figure 56. UNKNOWN ARTIST, ASSYRIAN (IX Century B.C.). A Winged God Holding a Goat and an Ear of Wheat, Relief from the Doorway of the Throne Room of the Palace of Assurnasirpal at Nimrud. London, British Museum.

Figure 57. UNKNOWN ARTIST, MYCENAEAN (c. 1570–1550 B.C.). Archers and Warriors Fighting Lions, Inlaid in Gold, Silver, and Black Niello in Bronze Dagger. Athens, National Archaeological Museum.

Figure 58. UNKNOWN ARTIST, GREEK (C. 480 B.C.). Heracles, from the Pediment of the Temple of Aphaia at Aegina. Munich, Glyptothek.

Greek artists were the first in the ancient world to work toward a full understanding of the anatomy of the human body. One can trace through the centuries the change—not altogether an improvement—in the rendering of the athletic figure. From the formality of the sixth and fifth centuries B.C., seen in the "Heracles" of *Figure 58,* they moved to concern for the texture of flesh and details of appearance at the end of the third century B.C., evident in the "Dying Gaul" (*Figure 59*). The taste of the Etruscans and the Romans followed that of the Greeks, and for many centuries it was taken for granted that artists must know and represent the human body correctly.

But in the early centuries of the Christian era, people in the Mediterranean world became more concerned with the spirit of man than with his body. Artists gave less attention to problems of anatomical structure and existence in space and more to

Figure 59. UNKNOWN ARTIST, GREEK (III Century B.C.). Dying Gaul. Rome, Capitoline Museum.

Figure 60. UNKNOWN ARTIST, BYZANTINE (XII Century). St. Basil, St. Gregory, and St. John Chrysostom, Mosaic. Palermo, Palatine Chapel.

the suggestion of inner being (*Figure 60*). Eyes look out at the spectator, enlarged and heavily outlined in solemn, flat faces. Bodies, considered important merely as the dwelling place for the soul, become flat and unreal. Draperies show little of the limbs beneath, but are conventionalized into patterns. Rich materials—gold and precious stones—reflect the luxury of the court of Byzantium, and mosaic with its glittering bits of colored glass or stone creates a kind of magic of its own.

Elongated bodies patterned with decorative lines continued in the Romanesque style which dominated Europe in the eleventh and twelfth centuries (*Figure 61*). But Gothic artists turned again to the world around them. These men of the thirteenth and fourteenth centuries saw all nature as mirroring the goodness of God, and therefore to be represented in works of art. The human figure grew rounder, its proportions more nearly correct. Yet the spirituality of the Byzantine tradition continued in the faces and postures of saints who seem almost to quiver with inner excitement (*Figure 62*).

Figure 61. UNKNOWN ARTIST, FRENCH (XII Century). Isaiah. Souillac, West Portal of Church.

Figure 62. UNKNOWN ARTIST, FRENCH (XIII Century). St. Theodore. Chartres, South Portal of the Cathedral.

Like the artist of the Middle Ages, the Oriental also interpreted the body so as to transmit inner meaning. A representation of Buddhist deity with eyes cast down, figure and draperies in smooth curves, embodies the idea of contemplation (*Figure 63*). The "Angry Actor" (*Figure 64*), an eighteenth-century Japanese print, is so confused anatomically that one wonders how his body works, but his anger is perfectly clear. This is indicated by the squares standing on their corners, by the sharp contrasts of dark and light, by the jagged contour against the background with hardly a line parallel to the frame.

Figure 63. UNKNOWN ARTIST, CHINESE (V Century). Maitreya. Boston, Museum of Fine Arts.

Figure 64. TORII KIYOMASU, JAPANESE (XVIII Century). Angry Actor, Woodcut. Cambridge, Fogg Art Museum, Harvard University, Ross Collection.

Figure 65. ANTONIO POLLAIUOLO, ITALIAN (1433-1498). Martyrdom of St. Sebastian. London, National Gallery.

The Renaissance study of space—perspective and foreshortening—which we discussed in Chapter 4, went hand in hand with an equally earnest study of human anatomy. In spite of the ban of the Church, bodies were dissected, and the shape and function of bones, muscles, and nerves were explored. Antonio Pollaiuolo devoted himself to rendering the body in tense action, to mastering and transmitting through both painting and sculpture a feeling of energy. This he expressed in modeling, and also in contour. Run your eye slowly along the edges of his figures; you can find yourself feeling a sympathetic tension in your own muscles. In the "Martyrdom of St. Sebastian" (which, incidentally, takes place against a fine landscape background) Pollaiuolo presented a nude accurately, and also, in the executioners, studies of figures in different postures (*Figure 65*). The standing bowman on the left shows from the front the same pose that we see to the right from the rear. The men bending over their crossbows are really one model seen from different angles.

By the end of the fifteenth century great artists all over Europe were studying the anatomy of the human figure. Artists like Leonardo da Vinci and Michelangelo made preliminary drawings in the nude of figures that were to be painted clothed to be sure that the body structure was correct under the drapery (*Figure 66*).

Figure 66. MICHELANGELO BUONAROTTI, ITALIAN (1475–1564). Studies for the Libyan Sibyl on the Sistine Chapel Ceiling. New York, The Metropolitan Museum of Art, Joseph Pulitzer Bequest.

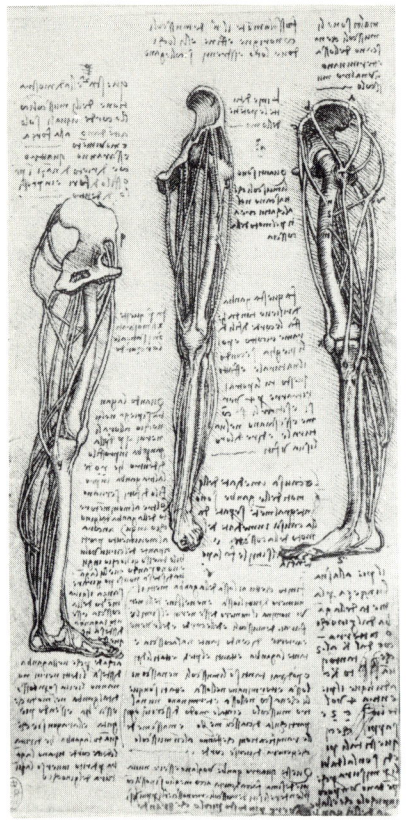
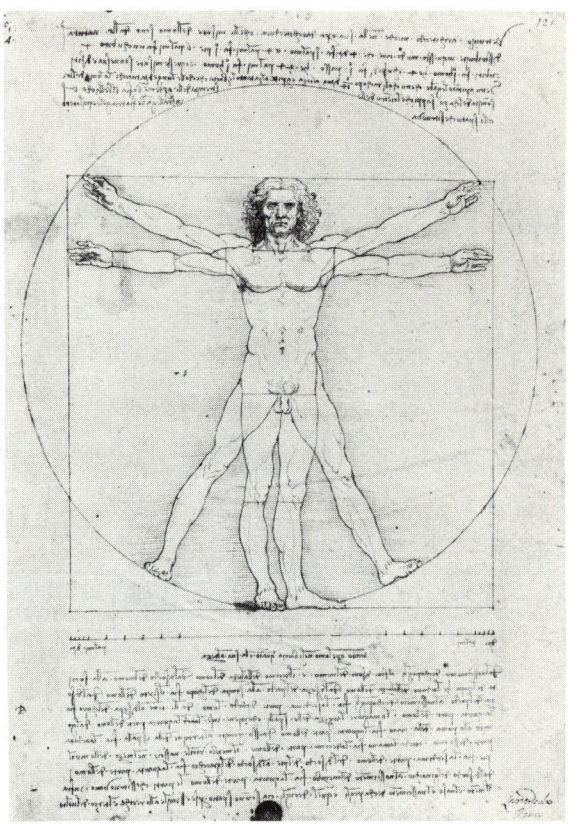

Figure 67. LEONARDO DA VINCI, ITALIAN (1452–1519). Drawing: Left Leg in Three Positions. Windsor, Royal Library.

Figure 68. LEONARDO DA VINCI, ITALIAN (1452–1519). Study of Human Proportions. Venice, Accademia.

Leonardo spent much of his life working on a "Treatise on Anatomy" in which he planned to include drawings of bones, muscles, and nerves (*Figure 67*). He also wrote at length on the relative proportions of the body. "From the chin to the nostrils is a third part of the face.... The space between the eyes is equal to the size of one eye," he states, and goes on to many comparisons. "If you set your legs so far apart as to take a fourteenth part from your height, and you open and raise your arms until you touch the line of the crown of the head ... the center of the circle formed by the extremities of the outstretched limbs will be the navel, and the space between the legs will form an equilateral triangle." The drawing accompanying the text makes the meaning clear (*Figure 68*). This is Leonardo's "man of perfect proportions," the ideal man fitted into the abstract order of the universe as represented by geometry. We realize, of course, that all people are not shaped the same way, that Leonardo's "man" is his own creation, and that individuals offer infinite variations from the rules which he laid down, but this Italian ideal of human proportions became the fashion throughout Europe. Albrecht Dürer, although he began by drawing in the German style of spare, angular figures, changed to the well-muscled Italianate type. Like Leonardo, he saw in the figure of man analogies to geometry, and his notebooks show him even resolving the human figure into geometric solids (*Figure 69*).

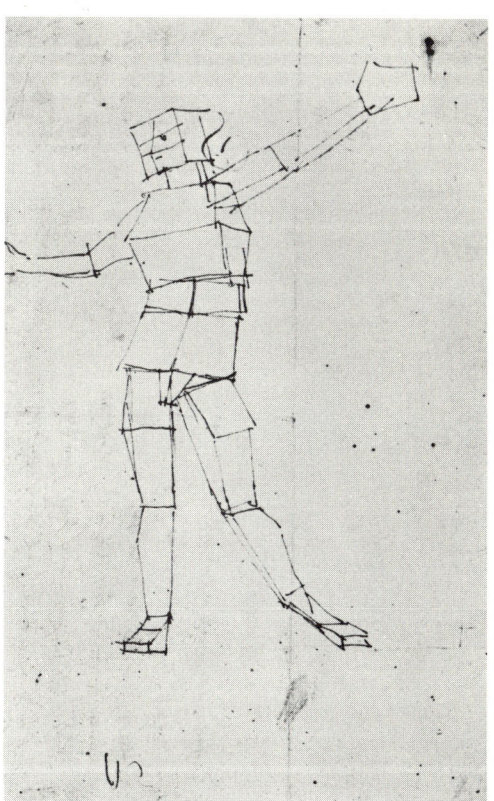

Figure 69. ALBRECHT DÜRER, GERMAN (1471–1528). Figure Composed of Stereometric Solids, Pen Drawing. Dresden, Sachsische Landesbibliothek.

Leonardo and Dürer derived their geometric simplifications from their study of anatomy. Other artists began with a block of stone or the trunk of a tree, and without formulated theory achieved comparable results. A figure from the Cyclades Islands in the Aegean Sea, dating from about 3000 B.C., has an oval for a head, a slab for a nose, a flattened cylinder for a neck, and a body basically rectangular (*Figure 70*). Similarly, in African sculpture we find the human body translated into shapes which have only a remote connection with human appearance (*Figure 71*).

Figure 70. UNKNOWN ARTIST, PRE-GREEK (C. 3000 B.C.). Figure of a Woman, from the Cyclades. Buffalo, Albright-Knox Art Gallery, Sherman S. Jewett Fund.

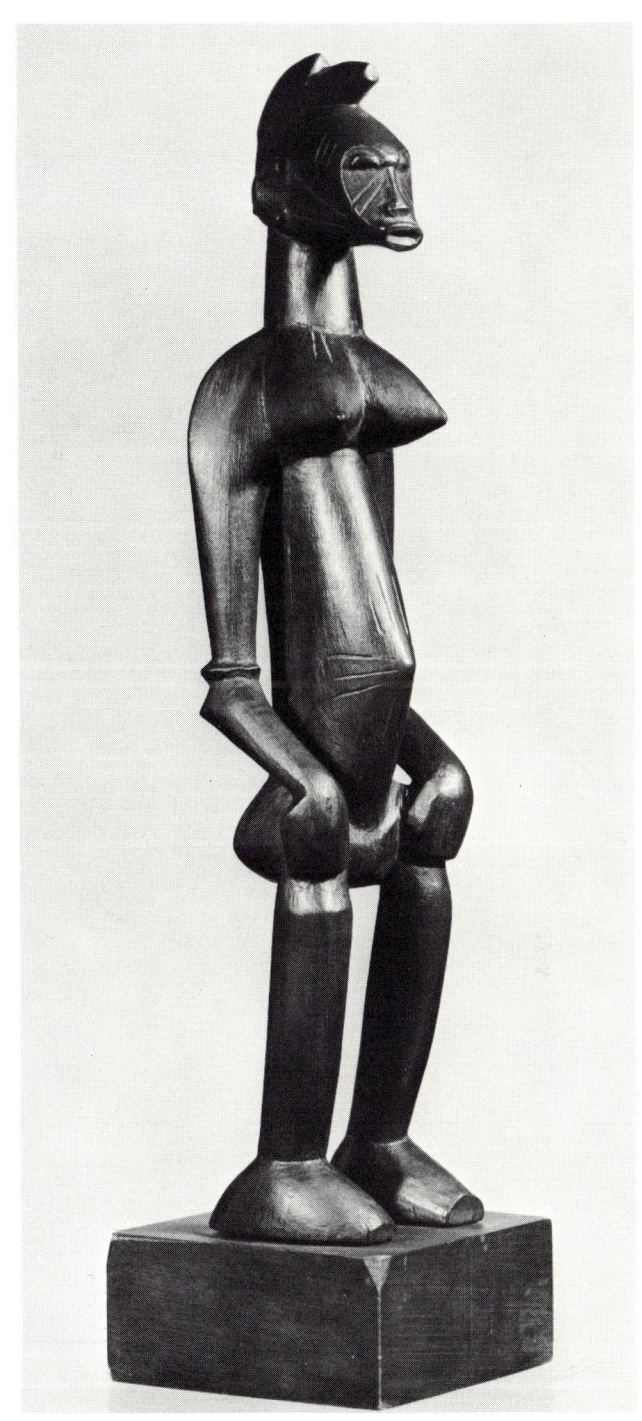

Figure 71. UNKNOWN ARTIST, AFRICAN. Female Figure from Ivory Coast, wood. New Haven, Yale University Art Gallery.

Figure 72. UNKNOWN ARTIST, AMERICAN INDIAN (TLINGIT). Totem Pole from Sitka, Alaska, wood. New York, Museum of the American Indian, Heye Foundation.

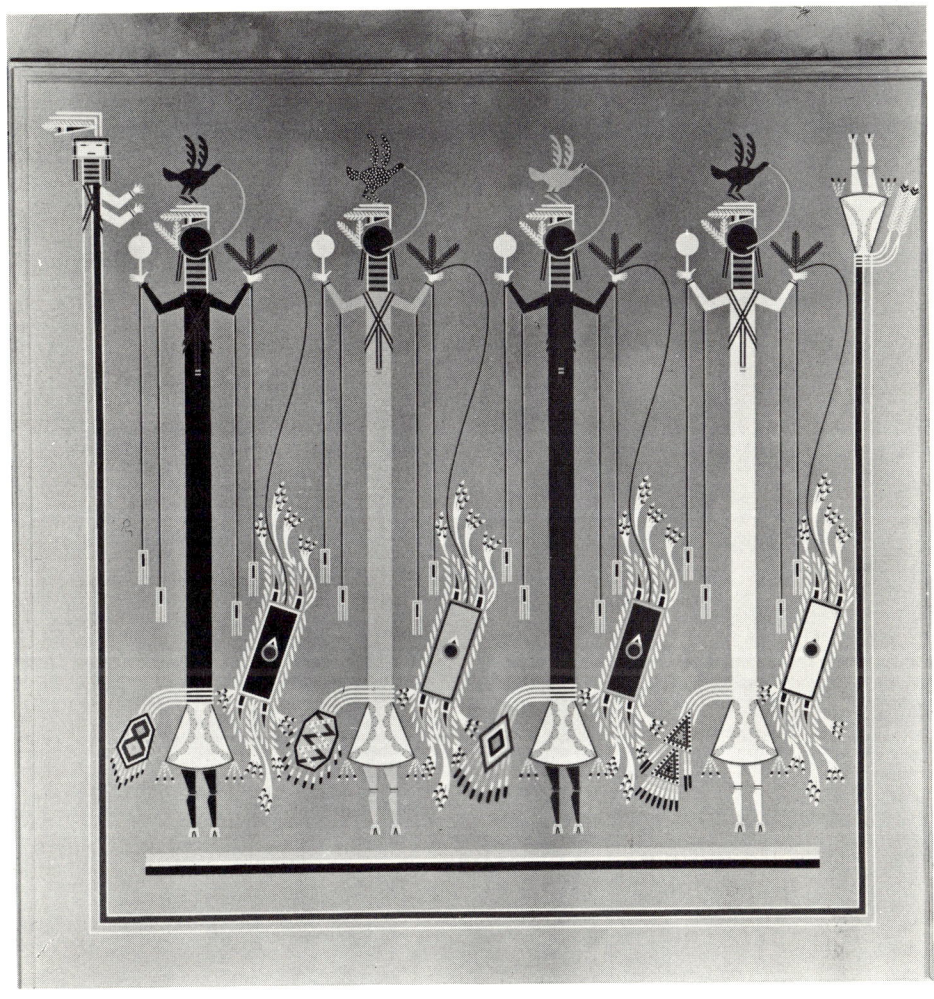

Figure 73. UNKNOWN ARTIST, AMERICAN INDIAN (NAVAJO). Four Ceremonial Dancers, Sand Painting from the Night Chant. Santa Fe, New Mexico, Museum of Navajo Ceremonial Art.

We are familiar also with totem poles (*Figure 72*), with figures from ancient Mexico, with the work of the American Indians (*Figure 73*).

So again, the artist can use the body, as he did landscape and perspective, to transmit ideas, some of which may require that he show anatomy correctly while others may not.

6. The Artist Creates His Picture

In the last few chapters we have noticed the way in which people of different periods and cultures have represented landscape, space, and the human figure. Often the artist himself did not have the conscious choice of how he would paint or carve. His methods grew out of the culture into which he was born, in which he was trained. It would not have occurred to an early Egyptian, for instance, to try to make a figure look round, modeled in light and shade and casting a shadow. He accepted the conventional profile rendering, probably never questioned it, and within the conventions could exercise skill and some originality.

In cultures which encourage individual originality, such as those of ancient Greece or Rome, of the Renaissance, or of our own times, the artist has more choice. He may, as the Egyptian artist did, continue to use the art of the past and at the same time work toward the expression of new ideas in new ways. In the Renaissance some of the greatest artists collected antique sculptures. But they were also stirred by a lively curiosity about the world of their own day. They shared in the scientific discoveries of the time, leading the way in fields of anatomy, geology, botany, and zoology, as well as in perspective, foreshortening, and effects of light and shade. Many of them observed the world around them with an extraordinary acuteness of vision matched by skill in setting down with pen or brush what they saw. Recording facts may be important, but great artists use their genius to transmit their ideas. They are individuals with the power to think, to experience, to feel, and to dream, and it is from these capacities, as well as from the skill of their fingers and their observation of the world, that their art springs. So the great artist may falsify his perspective, arrange his figures, make shadows fall where he wants them, eliminate, add, or distort, to secure his effects.

Figure 74. GIOVANNI DI PAOLO, ITALIAN (1402–1482). St. John the Baptist Leaves His Home to Go into the Wilderness. Chicago, Art Institute.

Giovanni di Paolo, a fifteenth-century Italian, used landscape to reinforce his story. He painted the life of John the Baptist in six scenes, in one of which John leaves his home to take up the life of an ascetic in the wilderness (*Figure 74*). He emerges from the gate at the left and appears again, halfway up the path, walking briskly into the mountains. But we know that John later was imprisoned and beheaded by Herod. Giovanni di Paolo opposes the rugged world of nature that John is entering to the orderly world of man that he is leaving behind. The ragged edge of the path and the sharp mountain

73

Figure 75. DOMENICO THEOTOCOPOULOS (called EL GRECO), SPANISH (C. 1547–1614). Christ's Agony in the Garden of Gethsemane. London, National Gallery.

peaks contrast with the neat, checkerboard fields slanting into the distance. The diagonals of the fields make sharp points that seem to thrust at John, and his martyrdom is also hinted by the dark red sky toward which he climbs.

The seventeenth-century Greek who became known as El Greco in Spain, where he spent most of his life, was fully able to paint naturalistically, but in his "Christ in the Garden of Gethsemane" he creates a strange, unreal landscape (*Figure 75*). The kneeling Christ is backed by a huge rock that repeats his shape, reminding us that Christ is often spoken of as a "rock." Above, back view, the elegantly patterned angel frames the cup, symbol of Christ's suffering and also of man's salvation. The sleeping apostles are enclosed in a curious egg-shaped swirl of mist, or perhaps a cave. They are shut away from the significance of the moment by more than their sleep, El Greco seems to say. They are not yet born into an understanding of the meaning of Christ. The Easter moon at the right is half hidden by clouds to suggest the spiritual storm that is going on and the evil intent of the shadowy soldiers below led on by Judas.

We have seen how light on figures, casting parts into shadow, gives solidity, creates the illusion of their existing in space. But when the source and direction of light is as hard to explain as in Tintoretto's "Moses Striking the Rock" (*Figure 76*), we realize that the artist is not at all concerned with copy-

Figure 76. JACOPO ROBUSTI (called TINTORETTO), ITALIAN (1512–1594). Moses Striking the Rock. Venice, Scuolo di San Rocco.

ing nature but is creating light and shade for his own purposes. Moses in the center looms dark against a light distance, the bright water, which flowed from the rock at the touch of his rod, arching over him. Light-edged clouds support a figure of God. The people in the foreground, composed in a half circle, reach up with jars and dishes to catch the water; their figures, arms, and legs weave into a sort of braid, light edges set off against dark, dark against light. This unnatural but masterly handling of light and shade brings order into the complex scene and gives it dramatic effect.

In quieter vein, and without disregarding the effect of light coming from the right, Titian used shadow to emphasize meaning. In his "Entombment of Christ" (*Figure 77*), the eyes of

Figure 77. TIZIANO VECELLI (called TITIAN), ITALIAN (1477–1576). The Entombment of Christ. Paris, Louvre.

Figure 78. REMBRANDT VAN RIJN, DUTCH (1606–1669). The Raising of Lazarus, Etching. New Haven, Yale University Art Gallery, Fritz Achelis Memorial Collection.

John, Mary Magdalene, and Mary the Mother are sunk into haggard depths; but even more meaningful is the shadow on the head, shoulders, and chest of Christ—the shadow of death made visible.

Rembrandt, in seventeenth-century Holland, is particularly famous for his handling of light. Nowhere does he use it more effectively than in his etching of "The Raising of Lazarus" (*Figure 78*). Against a dark, cavelike structure people crowd around Christ, some of them casting shadows, some not, while opposite, alone, drawn with few lines and making no shadow on the almost blank rock, Lazarus struggles back to life. From the crowded, shadowed world of man, faces yearn toward the

Figure 79. LEONARDO DA VINCI, ITALIAN (1452–1519). The Last Supper. Milan, Santa Maria della Grazie.

light of the miracle. Jesus links the two worlds, his figure lightly drawn, almost luminous.

Perspective, as we saw in Chapter 4, is a tool for the representation of depth in space. But it, too, can emphasize meaning. In the "Last Supper" (*Figure 79*) Leonardo da Vinci painted the walls and ceiling of the room receding to a vanishing point which coincides with the head of Christ. It is both vanishing point and the focal point of the whole composition. The window further emphasizes him, as does the arc above it, which is also centered on his head. In addition, Leonardo worked out a geometric organization for the picture, in which the figure of Christ is an equilateral triangle, his head the apex, his hands the two points. This triangle expresses the completeness of Christ, and is also a symbol of the Trinity. The only other triangular figure is that of Judas, to our left, a right triangle resting on one side, its hypotenuse slanting away from the Christ figure. Thus Leonardo withdraws Judas, the betrayer, from Christ, the betrayed. The other apostles gesture violently, yet

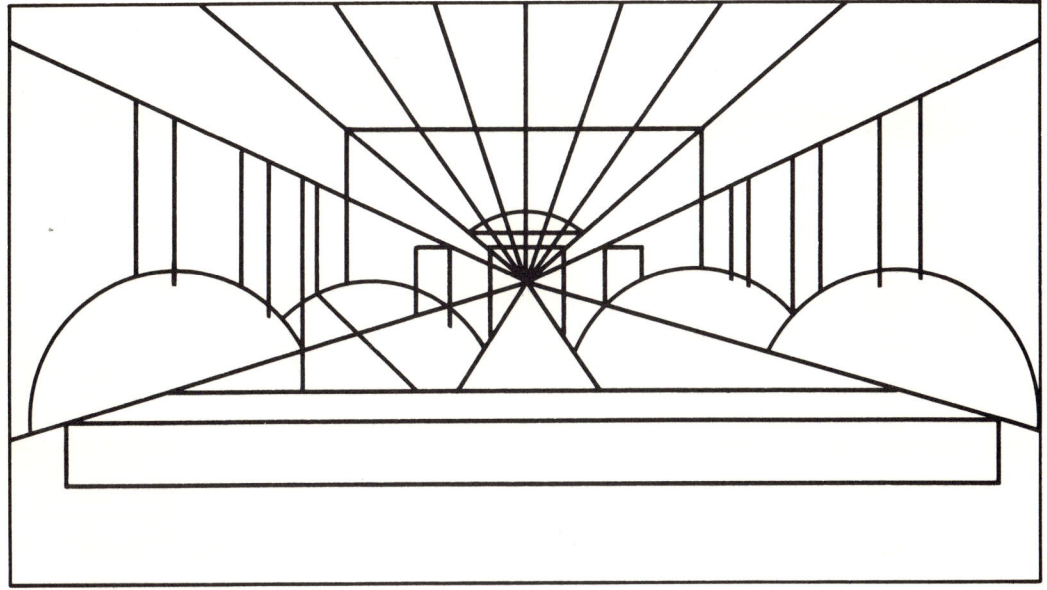

Figure 80. Diagram of the perspective composition of Leonardo's *Last Supper*.

are restrained in semicircular groups, emphasizing their inability to break out of the framework of their lives and engage in positive action. Christ is set apart, alone in the middle. Thus scientific perspective and geometric order serve the meaning of the picture (*Figure 80*).

Raphael, a contemporary of Leonardo but younger, used perspective similarly to interpret a more complicated theme (*Figure 81*). Although called "The School of Athens," the painting is more accurately "A Reconciliation of Plato and Aristotle." These two ancient Greek philosophers were much admired in the Renaissance. The elder, Plato, dealt with the relations between man and God; the younger, Aristotle, wrote his *Ethics* on relations among men. Plato points upward, a statue of Apollo, god of inspiration, occupying a niche to his right. Aristotle gestures outward, his side of the painting presided over by a statue of Athena, goddess of wisdom. Around and below them are men who have demonstrated these masters' philosophies, either in theory or in practice. The theoreticians

Figure 81. RAPHAEL SANZIO, ITALIAN (1483–1520). School of Athens. Rome, Vatican, Stanza della Segnatura.

stand on the upper level, the practitioners on the lower, with the man on the steps linking the two. He probably represents medicine which, in the Renaissance, was considered to be the science that held body and soul in balance, and was intermediate between theory and practice. The scene is set in a great room opening into a barrel-vaulted hall. The curious alternation of enclosure and openness in the vault suggests the finite world of man and also the infinite space of God. The two philosophers are emphasized by their central position, and by being placed against the open sky. The vanishing point for the receding walls and floor falls exactly in the middle between the two men, separating them, but at the same time they are tied together by the emphatic repetition of the arches. Thus Raphael indicates the separateness of the two philosophies within an embracing unity.

In Chapter 5 we looked at works from Greece and the Renaissance in which artists were searching for a complete understanding of human anatomy, while in other cultures anatomical accuracy was of no concern. But often in the very cultures that *were* interested in accuracy, intentional distortion occurs. The Greek artist who painted the foot race on a vase of the sixth century B.C. (*Figure 82*) had much still to learn about anatomy, but when he made the heads small and emphasized the hips and legs he was clearly distorting intentionally. Heads matter little in a foot race. It is the rhythmic movement of the legs, accented by the arms, that counts. The artist even stretched

Figure 82. UNKNOWN ARTIST, GREEK (VI Century B.C.). Panathenaic Foot Race, Black Figured Amphora. New York, The Metropolitan Museum of Art, Rogers Fund, 1914.

Figure 83. THÉODORE GÉRICAULT, FRENCH (1791–1824). Horse Race at Epsom. Paris, Louvre.

the back leg of each figure, making it longer than the bent leg to give a sense of speeding forward.

Some twenty-five centuries later, called upon to paint a horse race, the Frenchman Théodore Géricault lifted all four feet of all the horses off the ground at once (*Figure 83*), stretching the forelegs forward, the hind legs back, in a totally impossible position. How better could he express the speed and the neck-and-neck straining toward a goal?

El Greco, though considered a Spanish painter, was born in Crete, where flat, elongated Byzantine saints decorated the walls of churches. Many of El Greco's paintings show people of normal proportions, but when he wanted to emphasize spiritual qualities, he, like his Byzantine forebears, lengthened and distorted. His "St. John the Baptist" stretches upward against the sky (*Figure 84*), his body well-muscled but impossibly elongated. Light flickers over it. The small head is supported on a strong neck, the fingers are long and slender. John's turbulent life and death are also suggested by the bright and ominous clouds.

Figure 84. DOMENICO THEOTOCOPOULOS (called EL GRECO), SPANISH (c. 1547–1614). St. John the Baptist. San Francisco, M. H. de Young Memorial Museum.

Figure 85. THOMAS GAINSBOROUGH, ENGLISH (1727–1788). Portrait of Miss Evans. Buffalo, Albright-Knox Art Gallery.

Portraiture is a branch of painting in which accuracy of likeness is usually a first requirement. But many artists intentionally distort in order to tell something about their sitter that is more important than likeness. "Miss Evans" (*Figure 85*) undoubtedly had a long narrow face, but in his portrait of her, Thomas Gainsborough has extended the nose and elongated the oval of the face, has stretched out the neck and the torso, and thus accented the elegance and aristocracy of his subject.

Distortion, too, has always been a familiar tool of caricature. Through the centuries artists have made caricatures to attract attention, to point up an abuse or a human foible, or for pure humor. A tired and discouraged choirmaster (*Figure 86*) was carved by an unknown German in the sixteenth century, sitting disconsolate on the arm of a choir stall. Among the

Figure 86. UNKNOWN ARTIST, GERMAN (XVI Century). Choir Director, Wood Carving from a Choir Stall. Thann (Alsace), Church of St. Theobald.

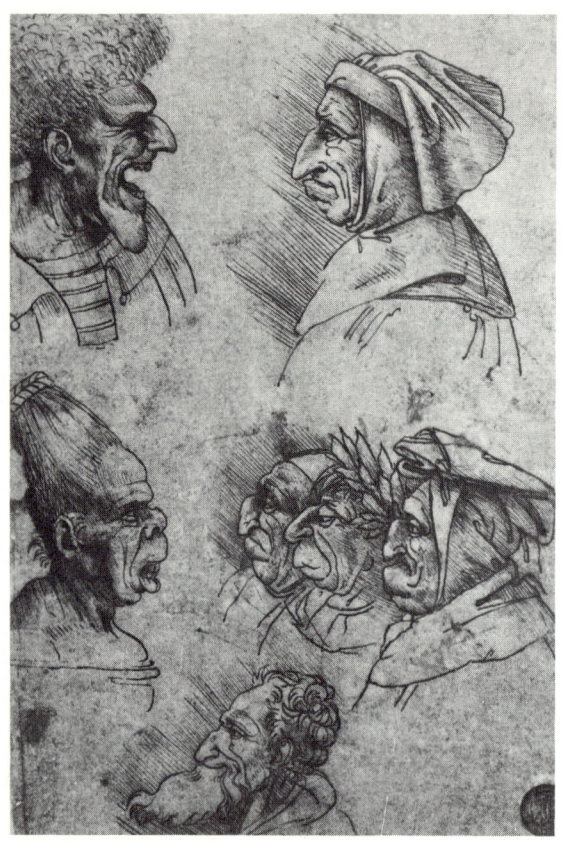

Figure 87. LEONARDO DA VINCI, ITALIAN (1452–1519). Caricatures, Drawing. Venice, Accademia.

many studies of facial expression by Leonardo da Vinci are some exaggerated caricatures (*Figure 87*). William Hogarth pointed up the abuses in the law courts of his eighteenth-century England by drawing pompous, bored, and drowsy lawyers (*Figure 88*). Honoré Daumier, the greatest caricaturist of nineteenth-century France, satirized sharply and effectively the political and social abuses of his time. And sometimes he indulged in pure humor, as in his "Hot Bath" (*Figure 89*).

These are some of the ways in which artists have brought their ideas to the attention of their audience. The skill, the ingenuity, the variety in methods of presentation are an endless source of surprise and pleasure to the spectator. They are the very essence of originality in art.

Figure 88. WILLIAM HOGARTH, ENGLISH (1697–1764). The Bench, Cambridge, Fitzwilliam Museum.

Figure 89. HONORÉ DAUMIER, FRENCH (1808–1879). The Hot Bath, Lithograph.

7. The Artist in the Twentieth Century

Probably all the departures from the photographic rendering of appearance that we noticed in the last chapter are perfectly acceptable to us. We enjoy the skillful use of landscape to reinforce the meaning of a scene. The great masters' handling of light and shade is so effective that it does not occur to us to object to its inaccuracy. We admire the perspective of Leonardo and Raphael. We accept El Greco's elongated figures. Readers of comic strips and viewers of movie cartoons as we are, we certainly take in stride the exaggerations of caricature. Why, then, are we so often baffled by the distortions, the exaggerations of the art of our own times? Why is it so different from the art of the past?

One might answer with another question: *Is* it so different? Are not the artists of today doing what great artists have always done—transmitting their ideas about the world through visual images? Is the difference between their works and those of the past partly due to the fact that ideas have changed and that the old images no longer have meaning?

Perhaps the fault is with us; we have not moved along as fast as the artists; we are trying to see our new world in the old way instead of opening our minds and spirits to the impact of the new.

It would take many chapters to point out the significant changes that have occurred in the world in the last century or two, but let us consider a few. Think, for instance, of the development of methods of transportation. For countless centuries the fastest man could go was on horseback or in a sailing ship.

Today we have locomotives, cars, planes, rockets, speedboats, and even hydrofoils. Think of the change in lighting that electricity has brought about. Think of the multiplication of reading matter—books, magazines, newspapers—the speeded communication through telephone, radio, television, the increased wealth and education that make these media available and meaningful to people. Think of the new world opened up by new instruments for seeing, such as telescopes and microscopes. Think of the wonderful machine we spoke of at the beginning of this book: the camera. With the invention of the camera, exact mechanical recording of appearance became possible. Artists were freed from any need to record. They could devote themselves to painting solely for the sake of transmitting ideas. They could experiment with colors, shapes, lines, seeking to express something more than exact representation. Furthermore, with the camera a world of new visual experiences became available, providing the artist with new images and stimuli. Microscopic and wide-angle lenses, high-speed film, movies and slow-motion films make a record of things and movements beyond the capacity of the normal human eye.

Another contribution of the camera is that through photography and color reproduction anyone anywhere can know (if it has been reproduced) every work of art that has ever been made. An artist used to travel from one city to another to see the paintings of other artists. Now, without leaving his home, he can see in reproduction what has been produced in the past, what is being done in the present. Reproductions are not substitutes for originals—but at least through reproduction the artist can see and learn of other styles, other forms of expression. When one takes into account, then, the new view of the world that comes with speed of travel, new knowledge that comes with rockets and spaceships, new information about the world around us through microscopes and cameras, new contacts between peoples through telephone, television, and pub-

Figure 90. CLAUDE MONET, FRENCH (1840–1926). Madame Monet under the Willows, 1880. Washington, National Gallery of Art, Chester Dale Collection.

lications, artists must inevitably paint new subjects in new ways.

In looking at the art of the last hundred years we will limit ourselves to the same subjects we have been studying in the art of the more distant past: landscape, space, the human figure.

Landscape of the early nineteenth century was, as we have seen (Chapter 3, *Figures 25-27*), essentially representational, concerned with space, distance, and the facts of the view. Shortly after 1850, inspired partly by the new scientific study of light and optics, artists concluded that what we see is not objects but light reflected from objects. Painters, named by a newspaper reviewer "impressionists," used dabs of bright color side by side, which the eye of the spectator automatically mixed as he looked at the painting from a distance (*Figure 90*). Since what they were painting was light, and since light changes every hour of the day, every month of the year, the impressionists often painted the same view over and over again at different times of day, or in different seasons. The artist submerged his own mind and spirit, turned himself into an eye in order to record what he saw.

Édouard Manet, Claude Monet, Pierre Renoir, and the other young Frenchmen who developed the theories of impressionism, suffered ridicule and abuse from a public used to the quiet color and smooth surfaces of the art of the past. But their investigation of color and light contributed enormously to the fresh and brilliant hues characteristic of much painting of recent years.

These very men soon turned away from the exact representation of light to an art which expressed more of their feeling about the world. They and their followers kept the bright color, using it, however, to express the excitement of sun, warmth and growth in spring, or of rain and storm. They laid on the paint in thick dabs, often using the direction and shape of the brushstrokes to enrich their effects. Vincent van Gogh, in his

Figure 91. VINCENT VAN GOGH, DUTCH (1853–1890). The Olive Orchard, 1889. Washington, National Gallery of Art, Chester Dale Collection.

"Olive Orchard" (*Figure 91*), painted trees that writhe and twist as though in an agony of growth and vitality. Maurice de Vlaminck painted streets and trees, windswept with storm, their details obliterated by broad paint strokes, the whole lighted by a lurid glow (*Figure 92*). In gayer vein, Oskar Kokoschka painted a "View of the Thames, London" (*Figure 93*), enlivened by broad accents of bright paint, a sunset sky suffusing the whole with light. What matter if the river is unnaturally wide, if the bridges are incorrect? The painting reflects his delight in the scene. We call these works *expressionist*—the presen-

Figure 92. MAURICE DE VLAMINCK, FRENCH (1876–1958). Winter Landscape, 1916–1917. New York, Museum of Modern Art.

Figure 93. OSKAR KOKOSCHKA, AUSTRIAN (1886–   ). View of the Thames, London, 1925–26. Buffalo, Albright-Knox Art Gallery.

tation of the artist's *feeling about* the view rather than the mere record of what he sees.

But some of the impressionists turned in another direction. They felt that the importance of landscape lay in its structure, its permanence; the exact effect of sunlight on a field at a certain time of day in a certain season might be interesting to observe and record, but what mattered was that the field was there, to be planted and harvested, in sun or rain, winter or summer. They were interested in its enduring qualities. Georges Seurat changed the impressionists' dabs of color into precise dots. He constructed his landscapes almost as though they were made with blocks. In his "Bathers" (*Figure 94*) each figure is solid and settled securely so that people and landscape give the feeling they belong together. The lasting characteristics of

Figure 94. GEORGES SEURAT, FRENCH (1859–1891). The Bathers, 1883–84. London, National Gallery.

Figure 95. PAUL CÉZANNE, FRENCH (1839–1906). Landscape with Rocks, c. 1896. London, National Gallery.

landscape rather than the transitory ones were similarly emphasized by Cézanne, who also had begun as an impressionist. Landscape to him was something that you tramp through, experiencing step by step. But the painting was not to look like an open window; it was on canvas and made of paint. Cézanne let the canvas show through here and there so you would not forget it. Your journey into the painting (*Figure 95*) is measured by blocklike brushstrokes, vertical and horizontal, designating the rocks and houses that you pass. The depth in space is limited by the mountain which seems to tip forward to create a positive end to the distance. Its curve repeats and reverses the

Figure 96. GEORGES BRAQUE, FRENCH (1882–1963). Houses at L'Estaque, 1908. Berne, Switzerland, Collection of Hermann Rupf.

curve of the road in the foreground. Perspective is not a matter of vanishing point but of colors carefully chosen. The greatness of the painting lies in its structure, in the way in which shapes and masses fit together as logically as the stones of a bridge. You react to the painting with your mind.

A next step in this intellectual concept of landscape came

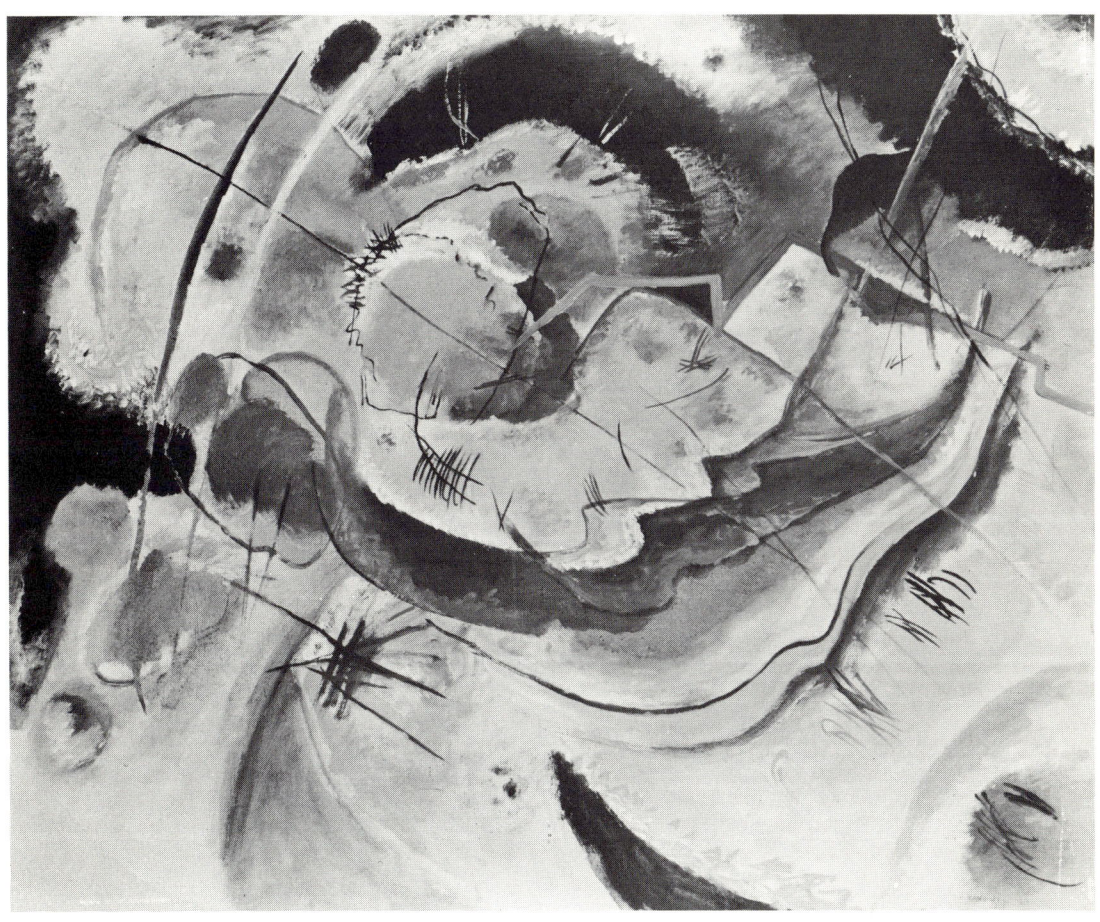

Figure 97. WASSILY KANDINSKY, RUSSIAN (1866–1944). Improvisation, 1914. Philadelphia Museum of Art, Louise and Walter Arensberg Collection.

with the so-called cubists, who broke up objects and spaces into geometric shapes which they felt offered a visual parallel to the order of the physical world (*Figure 96*).

Both types of landscape, the expressionist and the cubist, led into complete abstraction—on the one hand that of Kandinsky (*Figure 97*), whose paintings transmit light and life through glowing, exploding color areas, and on the other that of Mondrian, who states that for him ultimate reality is expressed in the opposition of verticals and horizontals

Figure 98. PIET MONDRIAN, DUTCH (1872–1944). Composition, 1936. Philadelphia Museum of Art, Louise and Walter Arensberg Collection.

and in a carefully balanced asymmetry (*Figure 98*).

Vanishing-point perspective in the Renaissance was a way of creating the illusion of distance, and relating objects to each other in the space thus created. Space was mathematically calculated. But many a twentieth-century artist is more impressed with the mystery and terror of space. Giorgio de Chirico tried to transmit something of this in paintings which at first glance seem precise and obvious, but as you look become ominous, disturbing (*Figure 99*). What is this world with its impossibly long arcade, its light that casts shadow but has no warmth? Is the child real? What of the unexplained shadow beyond the building? We find ourselves uncomfortable in an uncanny stillness. Even more nightmare-like are the spaces of

Figure 99. GIORGIO DE CHIRICO, ITALIAN (1888–   ). Melancholy and Mystery of a Street, 1914. New Canaan, Collection of Mr. and Mrs. Stanley R. Resor.

Figure 100. KAY SAGE, AMERICAN (1898–1963). Danger, Construction Ahead, 1940. New Haven, Yale University Art Gallery.

Kay Sage, a surrealist. "Danger, Construction Ahead" is the title for this scene of a road precariously suspended between one fantastic world and another more remote and mysterious (*Figure 100*). We are fascinated by the detail and the clarity, and at the same time repelled by the uncanny light, the desert which is not really desert, the metallic rocks, and the threat of the unknown in this world beyond reality called *surrealist*.

The space of the surrealists is related to the atmospheric perspectives of the past. Very different is the creation of space through careful manipulation of the hue, shape, size, and intensity of color areas. In Jacques Villon's "Color Perspective" (*Figure 101*) the yellow area comes forward, and the other colors fall into specific positions in space so that the whole seems to have depth instead of being merely a flat color pattern.

Figure 101. JACQUES VILLON, FRENCH (1875–1963). Color Perspective, 1922. New Haven, Yale University Art Gallery, Collection of the Société Anonyme.

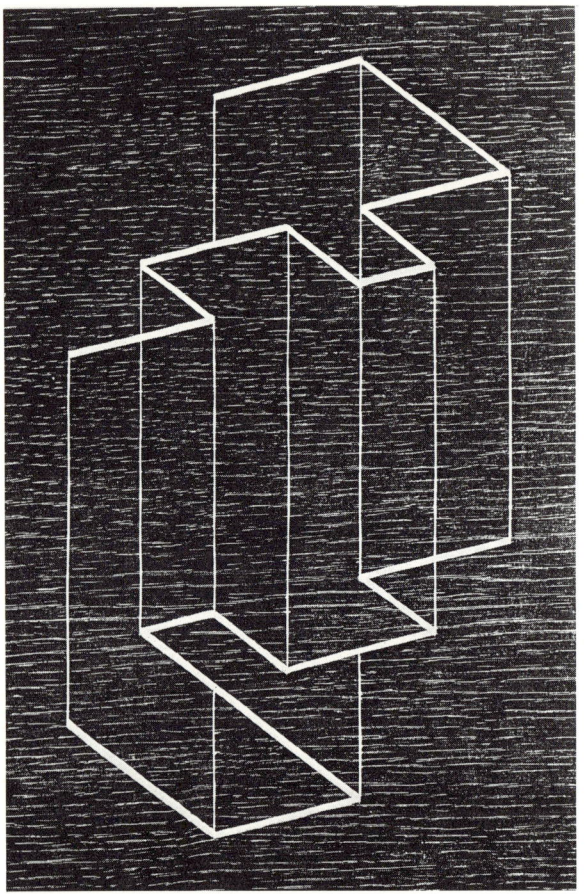

Figure 102. JOSEF ALBERS, GERMAN (1888–   ). Multiplex B, 1948. New Haven, Yale University Art Gallery.

Josef Albers, fascinated by the capacity of colors to take on space relations with each other, arbitrarily limited himself for a while to painting squares against squares. In a series called "Homage to the Square" he explored the interaction of colors in these precise areas. The central squares in these pictures drop back or come forward, and the other squares take up positions in space in relation to them. The edges vibrate, and the colors slip under or over each other. In another medium, white lines on a black ground, Albers created a similar sort of inner life in arrangements of parallel lines. As you fix your eyes on the lines in *Figure 102*, they flip from one position to another. They seem to have a kind of life of their own.

In painting the human figure, twentieth-century artists have shown little concern for accurate anatomy. It is as though, having mastered the structure of the human body, they were content to turn it over to the photographer and to the medical profession, while they devote themselves to other aspects of man. Paul Gauguin painted figures in a manner akin to the flat profile rendering of ancient Egypt. He enriched his palette with the warm browns and dark greens that he saw on a visit to Tahiti, and in "The Market" (*Figure 103*) he shows native women on a bench, their faces and figures, the background and trees rendered in flat areas of color. Influenced, perhaps,

Figure 103. PAUL GAUGUIN, FRENCH (1848–1903). The Market (Ta Matete), 1892. Basle, Art Museum.

Figure 104. HENRI MATISSE, FRENCH (1869–1954). Interior with Etruscan Vase, 1940. Cleveland Museum of Art, Hanna Fund.

by tapestries, Henri Matisse also enjoyed working with flat colors so balanced in the decorative pattern that each holds its position in space (*Figure 104*). For a while Pablo Picasso was strongly influenced by the sculptural solidity of Greek statues. "The Race" (*Figure 105*) is set in a simple landscape of sky, sea, and ground, within which pink figures as solid as stone move with astonishing abandon, their heads, arms, and legs thrusting outward like the spokes of a wheel rolling across the canvas. In the paintings of his "blue period," he was influenced by El Greco, elongating and patterning the figure in shallow space. Later, inspired partly by African sculpture, he broke up faces and figures into blocklike, cubist shapes (*Figure 106*).

Figure 105. PABLO PICASSO, SPANISH (1881-   ). The Race, 1923. Paris, Collection of the Artist.

Figure 106. PABLO PICASSO, SPANISH (1881-   ). Women with Pears, 1909. Chicago, Collection of Florene May Schoenborn and Samuel A. Marx.

Figure 107. PABLO PICASSO, SPANISH (1881–   ). The Three Musicians, 1921. New York, Museum of Modern Art, Mrs. Simon Guggenheim Fund.

Again, working in flat patterns, he created the delightful "Three Musicians" (*Figure 107*), their dog beneath their chairs with upraised tail, as though beating time to their oboe, guitar, and voice.

The effect of machines on man has been of interest and concern to many artists. Ben Shahn's "Welders" (*Figure 108*) crowd up against the rectangle of the canvas, strong and dominating human beings. They are men of muscle and skill, thoroughly in control of their tools. Reflected in their goggles are the girders they are erecting. Fernand Léger painted people who are dehumanized—hard, metallic. They have become robots without warmth or human emotions (*Figure 109*). The

106

Figure 108. BEN SHAHN, AMERICAN (1898–   ). Welders, 1943. New York, Museum of Modern Art.

Figure 109. FERNAND LÉGER, FRENCH (1881–1957). Three Women (The Breakfast), 1921. New York, Museum of Modern Art, Mrs. Simon Guggenheim Fund.

Mexican artist Diego Rivera was concerned with quite another aspect of the machine age—its effect on the social order. He painted enormous frescoes on themes of social reform. "The Night of the Poor" (*Figure 110*) shows weary peasants asleep, in contrast to a scene of people drinking champagne, "The Night of the Rich." By eliminating detail, reducing shadows, and drawing firm, clear outlines, he wins our sympathy for these simple folk.

Figure 110. DIEGO RIVERA, MEXICAN (1886–1957). The Night of the Poor (detail), 1926. Mexico City, Secretariat of Education.

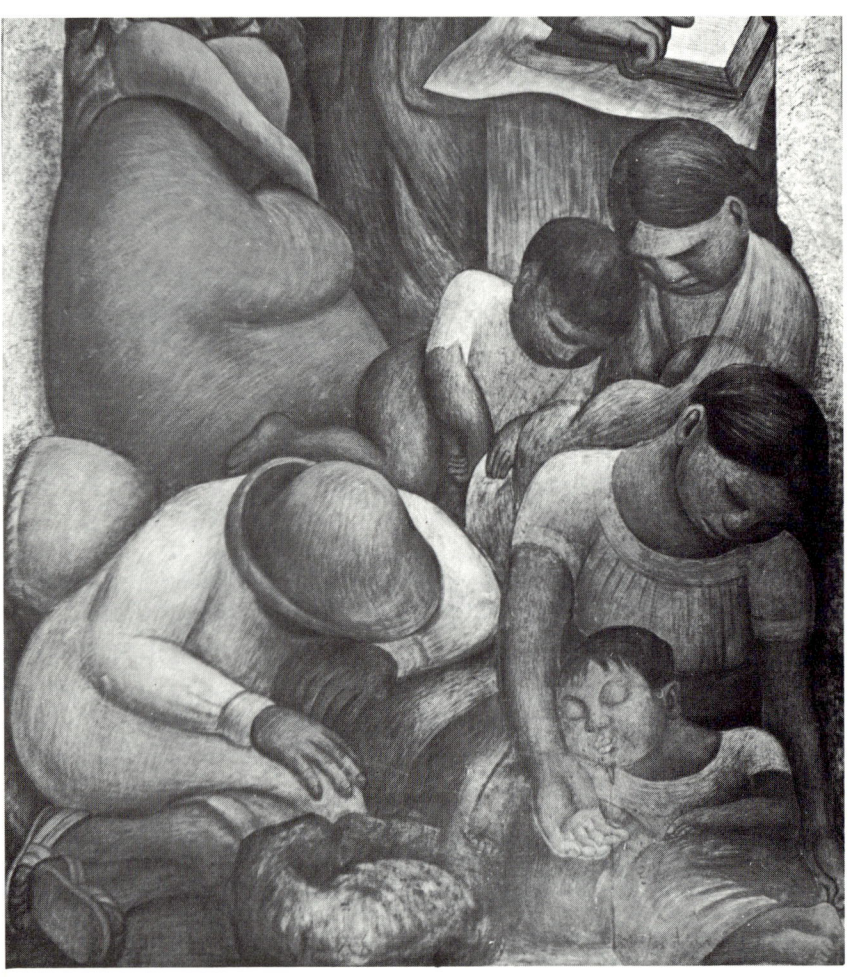

108

Figure 111. MARCEL DUCHAMP, FRENCH (1887–   ). Nude Descending a Staircase, No. 2, 1912. Philadelphia Museum of Art, Louise and Walter Arensberg Collection.

The focus on energy and movement in the modern world—difficult concepts to transmit visually—has given rise to new ways of painting figures in action. In his "Nude Descending a Staircase" (*Figure 111*), Marcel Duchamp attempted to translate into curves and angles the downward progress of a moving figure. The painting, exhibited in New York in 1913, raised a

Figure 112. KASIMIR MALEVICH, RUSSIAN (1878–1935). Scissors Grinder, 1912. New Haven, Yale University Art Gallery, Collection Société Anonyme.

furor which helped awaken the American public to progressive developments in art. The Russian painter Kasimir Malevich, in his "Scissors Grinder" (*Figure 112*), translated the vibrations of grinding into repeated hands, feet, and features, the idea of steel striking sparks against stone into blues, grays, and accents of orange. Joseph Stella, in his "Battle of Light, Coney Island" (*Figure 113*), wove the activities of an evening in an amusement park into a painted tapestry of movement—roller coasters, Ferris wheels, fireworks, flashing signs, strings of lights, and people—flickering in and out across the scene.

But now, as in the past, artists are concerned with the age-old aspects of man—his human nature essentially unchanged

Figure 113. JOSEPH STELLA, AMERICAN (1880–1946), Battle of Light, Coney Island, 1913. New Haven, Yale University Art Gallery, Collection Société Anonyme.

through time. In a series of figure studies for a "Crucifixion," Rico LeBrun, a naturalized American, created images inspired by the agony of men and women in World War II. His "Woman of the Crucifixion" is heroic in size, firm and unflinching, her dress and body flecked with red (*Figure 114*). She becomes an embodiment of steadfastness and compassion, a symbol of the involvement of all mankind in all human suffering.

Figure 114. RICO LEBRUN, AMERICAN (1900–1964). Woman of the Crucifixion, 1948. New Haven, Yale University Art Gallery, William C. Whitney Foundation.

Figure 115. MARC CHAGALL, RUSSIAN (1887–   ). Green Violinist, 1918. New York, Guggenheim Museum.

Both gay and melancholy is Marc Chagall's painting of a violinist (*Figure 115*). The artist drew the theme from a childhood memory of an uncle who was discovered one snowy night happily fiddling on the roof. Chagall's painting is as whimsical as his subject: the angular peasant figure balances precariously on the roof gables, green face and hand, orange violin and purple coat lifting the scene into the realm of fantasy where a listening horse and soaring human are equally at home.

Figure 116. ANDREW WYETH, AMERICAN (1917–   ). Young America, 1950. Philadelphia, Pennsylvania Academy of Fine Arts.

Compared to the extremes of expression that these men represent, Andrew Wyeth's realism is conservative, reminiscent of the Renaissance. In his hands exact detail is a means of expression. The America which he paints has a breadth and stillness that is curiously moving. His people are alone, self-contained, independent. "Young America" dominates the landscape, riding with an easy, youthful assurance, controlled, watchful, a successor of the westward pioneer, moving ever onward (*Figure 116*). The off-center balance crowding the bicycle toward the right gives a sense of continuing progress that is central to the subject.

There is no end to art. Even as you read, new paintings are being made, new ideas presented, new techniques developed. The abstract expressionists splash color on large canvases, sometimes controlling it with brush and palette knife, sometimes letting accident direct its spread and drip. Everyday objects—combs, bits of adhesive, brushes, metal or wood fragments—are brought together for new textures. "Pop" art, with a clarity deriving from the magazine page, grows out of commercialism, advertisement, and low-level communication in our radio, television, billboards, and comic strips. Monotony and variety, simplicity and complexity, conformity and originality—contradictions ever present in our modern life—are expressed in the multiple forms of our art.

Will it last? Who knows? What does it matter? Art is the expression of life. If life is varied and changing, rife with experiment, bringing new experiences and new knowledge, art must be, too. If some ideas are fruitful, some discarded, some meaningful for a time, then becoming obsolete, so are works of art. If some aspects of life interest some people and others stir their neighbors, so will tastes and interests vary in art. But the great artist has an awareness beyond that of most of us, is ever seeking for the deeper meaning of life, making it visible as he understands it. He can, if we will let him, guide us toward a wider and deeper understanding of ourselves and of our world.

Index

(Italic numbers indicate illustrations)

African, unknown, 69
Akhenaten and Nefertiti, 56
Albers, Josef, *102*
American Indian, unknown, 70, 71
Angry Actor, 62, *63*
Archers and Warriors Fighting Lions, 56, 57
Assyrian, unknown, 7, 37, 57
Austin, Darrel, 16, *17*

Babylonian, unknown, *8*
Baldung, Hans (Grün), *49*
Baptism of Christ, 22–23
Barye, Antoine Louis, *14*, 15–16
Bathers, The, 94
Battle of Light, Coney Island, *111*
Battle of Sam Romano, The, 46–47
Bench, The, 86, 87
Bierstadt, Albert, *30*
Blind Musician, 54, *55*
Braque, Georges, *96*
Bruegel, Pieter, 23, *25*
Byzantine, unknown, 9, 60

Caricatures, 86
Carpaccio, Vittore, *10*
Cézanne, Paul, *32*–*33*, *95*–*96*
Chagall, Marc, *113*
Chained Lion, *12*–*13*, 15
Chinese, unknown, *62*
Ch'ing-pien Mountains, The, *21*, 22
Chirico, Giorgio de, *98*–*99*
Choir Director, 85
Christ's Agony in the Garden of Gethsemane, 74–75
Church of St. Ignazio, 50–*51*
Color Perspective, 100, *101*
Composition, 97–*98*
Constable, John, *28*

Danger, Construction Ahead, 99–*100*
Daumier, Honoré, 86, *87*
Death of Saul at the Battle of Gilboa, 23, *25*
Delacroix, Eugène, 13–15, 16; *14*
Dioskourides, *40*–*41*
Drawing a Lute, 47–48
Duchamp, Marcel, *109*–110
Dürer, Albrecht, 10–*11*, *12*, 47–48, 49, 67–68
Duris, 38, *39*
Dying Gaul, *59*
Dying Lion, 6, 7, 8

Egyptian, unknown, *18*, *34*, *36*, *55*, 56
El Greco, 74–75, 82, *83*, 88, 104
Entombment of Christ, The, 76–77
Eyck, Hubert van, 22–*23*

Female Figure from Ivory Coast, 68, *69*
Female Mourners, *34*, 35
Figure Composed of Stereometric Solids, 67
Figure of a Woman, from the Cyclades, 68
Four Ceremonial Dancers, 71
French, unknown, *61*
Funeral Procession, *34*, 35

Gainsborough, Thomas, *84*, 85
Garden with Pond from the Tomb of Amenemheb, *18*, 19
Gauguin, Paul, *103*
Géricault, Theodore, *82*
German, unknown, *85*
Giovanni di Paolo, 73–74
Greek, unknown, 9, 39, *58*, *59*, *81*
Green Violinist, *113*
Groom Bewitched, The, 49

Harvesting Scene, 35–37; *36*
Heracles, *58*, 59

117

Heracles and Athena, 38, *39*
Hesi-Re, 54, *55*
Hobbema, Meindert, 26–27
Hogarth, William, 86, *87*
Horse Race at Epsom, *82*
Hot Bath, The, 86, *87*
Houses at L'Estaque, *96*, 97

Improvisation, 97
Inness, George, *29*
Interior with Etruscan Vase, *104*
Isaiah, 60, *61*

Kandinsky, Wassily, 97
Katsukawa, *52*, 53
King Assurnasirpal's Encampment and Stables, 37–38
Kiyomasu, Torii, 62, *63*
Kokoshka, Oskar, 92, *93*

Landscape, *18*, 19
Landscape with Rocks, 95–96
Last Supper, The, 78–79
LeBrun, Rico, *112*
Left Leg in Three Positions, 66
Léger, Fernand, 106, *107*
Leonardo da Vinci, 46, 65–68, 78–79, 86, 88; *66*
Lion Devouring a Rabbit, 13–15; *14*
Lion Drawn from Life, 11, *12*
Lion of St. Mark, *9*, 10
Lions, 12, *13*
Lion Walking, 15–16; *14*

Madame Monet under the Willows, *90*, 91
Madonna with Angels, 23, *24*
Maitreya, *62*
Malevich, Kasimir, *110*
Man Lying Down, *48*
Mantegna, Andrea, 49–50
Market, The, *103*
Martyrdom of St. Sebastian, 64–65
Matisse, Henri, *104*
Melancholy and Mystery of a Street, 98–99
Memling, Hans, 23, *24*
Michelangelo, 65
Minton, Robert H., *4*

Mondrian, Piet, 97–*98*
Monet, Claude, *90*, 91
Mont Sainte-Victoire from Les Lauves, *32–33*
Moses Striking the Rock, 75–76
Mount Corcoran, *30*, 91
Multiplex B, *102*
Murád, Ustád, 12, *13*
Mycenaean, unknown, 57

Night of the Poor, The, *108*
Nude Descending a Staircase, No. 2, *109*–110

Odysseus in the Land of the Cannibals, 20
Olive Orchard, The, *92*
On the Delaware River, *29*, 91

Panathenaic Foot Race, 81–*82*
Picasso, Pablo, *104*–106
Pollaiuolo, Antonio, 64–*65*
Portrait of Miss Evans, 84–*85*
Pozzi, Andrea, 50*051*
Pre-Greek, unknown, 68
Procession of Lions, 6, *8*, 15

Race, The, *104*–105
Raising of Lazarus, The, 77–78
Raphael Sanzio, 79–81, 88; *80*
Release of the Lion, *7*, 15
Rembrandt van Rijn, 77–78
Rivera, Diego, *108*
Roman, unknown, 20, *43*
Room from a Series of Scenes from the Life of St. James, *46*–47
Rousseau, Henri, *15*, 16
Ruysdael, Jacob van, 25–*26*

Sage, Kay, 99–*100*
St. Anthony Tormented by Demons, *44*, 45
St. Basil, St. Gregory, and St. John Chrysostom, *60*
St. Ignazio Entering Heaven, 50–*51*
St. James Led to Martyrdom, 49–*50*
St. Jerome in His Study, 10, *11*
St. Jerome Returning with the Lion, *10*
St. John the Baptist, 82, *83*
St. John the Baptist Leaves His Home to Go into the Wilderness, 73–*74*

St. Theodore, *61*
Sassetta, *44*, 45
School of Athens, The, 79–81; *80*
Scissors Grinder, *110*
Seated Lion, 8, *9*
Seurat, Georges, *94*
Shahn, Ben, 106, *107*
Sleeping Gypsy, The, *15*, 16
Starry Night, The, *31*
Stella, Joseph, *111*
Street Musicians, 40–41
Studies for the Libyan Sibyl on the Sistine Chapel Ceiling, *65*
Study of Human Proportions, *66*, 67

Three Musicians, The, *106*
Three Women (The Breakfast), 106, *107*
Tintoretto, 75–76
Titian, 76–77
Toba Sojo, *12–13*
Totem Pole from Sitka, Alaska, *70*, 71
Treatise on Anatomy, 66–67
Tung Ch'i-ch'ang, *21*, 22

Uccello, Paolo, *46–47*

Unknown artists, *see under area*

van Gogh, Vincent, *31*, 91–92
View of Buildings, 42–43
View of Haarlem from the Dunes, 25–26
View of the Thames, London, 92–94; *93*
Village in a Wood with Watermill, Among Trees, 26–27
Villon, Jacques, 100–*101*
Vlaminck, Maurice de, 92, *93*

Walking Lion, *4*, 5, 8, 15
Welders, 106–*107*
White Horse, The, *28*, 91
Winged God Holding a Goat and an Ear of Wheat, A, 56–57
Winter Landscape, 92, *93*
Woman of the Crucifixion, *112*
Women Airing Books, *52*, 53
Women with Pears, 104, *105*
Wrestlers, *36*, 37
Wrestling Scene, 38, *39*
Wyeth, Andrew, *114*

Young America, *114*
Young Lion in Moonlight, 16, *17*

About the Author

ALICE ELIZABETH CHASE *is Assistant Professor of the History of Art at Yale University, where she has also been Docent (museum lecturer) of the Yale Art Gallery for many years. As Docent, she directs the gallery's public education program and lectures on many phases of art to groups of all ages. She has published two previous books on painting for young people.*

Miss Chase was born in Ware, Massachusetts, and received her B.A. degree from Radcliffe College and her M.A. from Yale University. During a leave of absence from Yale, she served for a year as Curator of Education at the Brooklyn Museum. Miss Chase has traveled extensively in Europe, the Middle East, and Mexico.